Y0-BRL-482

Translation and Understanding

Translation and Understanding

Sukanta Chaudhuri

P
3Ø6
.C52
1999

OXFORD
UNIVERSITY PRESS

OXFORD
UNIVERSITY PRESS

YMCA Library Building, Jai Singh Road, New Delhi 110001

Oxford University Press is a department of the University of Oxford. It furthers the
University's objective of excellence in research, scholarship, and education
by publishing worldwide in

Oxford   New York

Athens   Auckland   Bangkok   Bogota   Buenos Aires   Calcutta
Cape Town   Chennai   Dar es Salaam   Delhi   Florence   Hong Kong   Istanbul
Karachi   Kuala Lumpur   Madrid   Melbourne   Mexico City   Mumbai
Nairobi   Paris   Sao Paolo   Singapore   Taipei   Tokyo   Toronto   Warsaw

with associated companies in

Berlin   Ibadan

© Oxford University Press 1999

ISBN 0 19 564877 3

I P F W

APR 2 3 2004

WITHDRAWN

HELMKE LIBRARY

Typeset by Sheel Arts, Delhi 110 092
Printed at Pauls Press, New Delhi 110 020
and published by Manzar Khan, Oxford University Press
YMCA Library Building, Jai Singh Road, New Delhi 110 001

Preface

The substance of this book was delivered as a series of lectures at the University of Alberta in October 1997. I must thank the University of Alberta and the Indo-Canadian Shastri Foundation for inviting me to Edmonton as Distinguished Visiting Professor. On a personal plane, I must thank Sumona and Shyamal Bagchee for their unfailing support and hospitality during my stay. I also warmly recall my interaction with Jonathan Hart, Jean MacIntyre and Gary Kelly.

I thank Subha Chakraborty Dasgupta and other members of the Department of Comparative Literature, Jadavpur University, for assisting me with books and advice. Indrani Das of Visva-Bharati generously provided me with information on Italian translations of Rabindranath Thakur.

A very short section of chapter 3 is taken from an article I contributed to the collection *Word for Word: Essays on Translation in Memory of Jagannath Chakravorty* (Calcutta: Papyrus, 1994). General inspiration for this book was afforded by activities under the Translation Studies section of the UGC Special Assistance (DSA) Programme of the Department of English, Jadavpur

University. I hope the programme will continue to encourage us to make translations and think about them.

SUKANTA CHAUDHURI

Department of English
Jadavpur University
July 1998

Contents

1

Translation and Cultural Encounter

The act of translation has traditionally been seen in a moral light. Opinion has differed down the ages as to whether the writing of poetry, or any other kind of 'original' text, involves exercising or imparting some species of moral virtue. But the translation of existing texts has commonly been viewed in ethically loaded terms: whatever the moral standing of the original, the translator is expected to adhere to it in a spirit whose definition is essentially moral.

The classic expression of this syndrome is in the recurrent appeals to 'truth' and 'fidelity'. Truth is a difficult concept. I will not wash my hands of it, but I will reserve it for later discussion. Fidelity, again, can be of many kinds; but the implication here is undoubtedly of sexual faith. (The point has been made by a number of women translators and scholars.[1]) The sense surfaces in the weary old sexist quip that a translation is like a woman, either beautiful or faithful but not both. As with a woman's change of partner, the departure of a translation from the original evokes the compelling suggestion of a threatening, subversive force, the infringement of set parameters of possession and authority. That pun is meaningful: translation can destabilize the protocol of signification whereby the author of an 'original' text claims precedence by a precarious and questionable process. Fearsome and fascinating things might happen if, like some indecorous Victorian lady, the reader begins to move, as she clearly does by turning translator.

The Bengali poet Jagannath Chakravorty saw the risk posed by translation to the integrity of the poet's persona:

> Translate me so that I seem
> Neither sea nor mountain,
> Neither summer nor winter,
> As though I were someone else, something else.

Chakravorty sees the danger as reductive: 'Tame me ... / Twist and bend the arrogant horns within me.'[2] But this fear of self-loss masks the deeper fear of being subsumed in a greater phenomenon, an impersonal, illimitable continuum of verbal process. This deeper fear is akin to the anguish of Donne's projected poet who hears a man 'set and sing' his song, thereby releasing the grief that his 'verse did restraine'.[3] What music can do, translation does as well. It transfers the ur-stuff of a formulated experience to a new medium with its own demands.

Translation can release an alternative, subversive potential of the text, turn it inside-out to bring its deconstructive factor to the fore. The new language draws out possibilities beyond the original writer's intention or awareness, possibilities he might have consciously rejected. Going beyond authorial intention, they might be possibilities that his own language would not admit but that are instilled in the new text by the structures of the target (or, as I would prefer to call it, 'host') language.

The process obviously works in negative as well—that is to say, by closing off possibilities that had existed in the original. As we cannot but know prominently since Derrida, the Greek *pharmakon* is both 'medicine' and 'poison'. So is the English *drug*, but the one word cannot fitly and uniformly render the other. Its use would be more misleading than the common though always questionable translator's resort of using different words at different points to render the same word in the source: in this case, to use the equivalents in the English translation of Derrida's own text, *remedy, recipe, poison, drug, philtre* etc. 'It is a difficulty,' says Derrida (and never let it be forgotten that I am citing him in translation),

inherent in [the] very principle [of translation], situated less in the passage from one language to another, from one philosophical language to another, than already, as we shall see, in the tradition between Greek and Greek; a violent difficulty in the transference of a nonphilosopheme into a philosopheme.[4]

In the most fundamental sense, 'the transference of a nonphilosopheme into a philosopheme' is what happens in every particle of every act of translation. The source text, a semiotic construct of indeterminate range, is negotiated by seizing on a feasible, tractable part of its range and imposing upon it a similar segment of another indeterminate construct in another language. The circle is sought to be squared, but the exercise demonstrates its own impossibility: we pass through a contextually restricted corridor from one expansive verbal system into another. Seen in this light, translation flings the text back into a vortex analogous to that from which the original writer had rescued it.

By a process analogous to Derridean *différance*—indeed a special version of it—translations endlessly extend and thus endlessly defer the implications of the original. Derrida's words in a different context are eminently applicable to the pursuit of equivalence in translation:

If totalization no longer has any meaning, it is not because the infiniteness of a field cannot be covered by a finite glance or a finite discourse, but because the nature of the field—that is, language and a finite language—excludes totalization. ... The movement of signification adds something, which results in the fact that there is always more, but this addition is a floating one because it comes to perform a vicarious function, to supplement a lack on the part of the signified.[5]

A translation is a binary of the original text. It extends its being; it threatens its being. The threat can take many forms, from inept mimicry to a manifestly richer compound; from reverting to the irresolutions the original had left behind, to achieving a synthesis it could not reach. But it is naive to assume, as I did in that last sentence, a linear valorized scale of formal progress from chaos to order. The irresolution might be masterly, the synthesis reductive; it is impossible to compare degrees or varieties of synthesis. The impossibility is more marked because the comparison is made across languages.

For the fundamental issue is not the encounter of two creative individuals but of two languages, two cultures, two paradigms of the mind; not even, really, two specific, individuated locations in mental space and time, but the deflected play of all that lies between and beyond.

Here is Pope's version of *Iliad* 15 : 458–77, where Zeus, protecting Hector, deflects and breaks Teucer's deadly arrow:

But *Hector* was not doom'd to perish then:
Th'all-wise Disposer of the Fates of Men,
(Imperial *Jove*) his present Death withstands;
Nor was such Glory due to *Teucer's* Hands.
At its full Stretch, as the tough String he drew,
Struck by an Arm unseen, it burst in two;

Down drop'd the Bow; the Shaft with brazen Head
Fell innocent, and on the Dust, lay dead.
Th'astonish'd Archer to great *Ajax* cries;
Some God prevents our destin'd Enterprize:
Some God, propitious to the *Trojan* Foe,
Has, from my Arm unfailing, struck the Bow,
And broke the Nerve my Hands had twin'd with Art,
Strong to impell the Flight of many a Dart.
   Since Heav'n commands it (*Ajax* made reply)
Dismiss the Bow, and lay thy Arrows by;
Thy Arms no less suffice the Lance to wield,
And quit the Quiver for the pond'rous Shield.
In the first Ranks indulge thy Thirst for Fame,
Thy brave Example shall the rest enflame,
Fierce as they are, by long Successes vain;
To force our Fleet, or ev'n a Ship to gain,
Asks Toil, and Sweat, and Blood: Their utmost Might
Shall find its Match — No more: 'Tis ours to fight.[6]

Here now is the same passage as rendered by E. V. Rieu, founder-editor of the Penguin Classics (which, however, has since withdrawn Rieu's *Iliad* and revised his *Odyssey*):

Zeus, who is too wary to be caught, was looking after Hector and had kept an eye on Telamonian Teucer. He robbed him of his triumph by breaking the twisted cord of his strong bow as he was taking aim at his man. The arrow with its load of bronze went wandering off, and the bow fell from his hand. Teucer shuddered and turned to his brother with an oath. 'Some evil power,' he exclaimed, 'is spoiling everything we try to-day! He has knocked the bow out of my hand and broken a fresh string that I bound on this morning to carry the many arrows that I meant to shoot.'

'Well, my friend,' said the great Telamonian Aias, 'you might as well put down your bow and all those arrows, now that some god who is annoyed with us has made them of no use. Lay your hand on a long spear instead, sling a shield on your shoulder, and so meet the enemy and give a lead to our men. The Trojans may have beaten us, but we can at least show them once more how we can fight, and make them pay dearly for the well-found ships.'[7]

Pope's use of the Latinate 'Jove' for Zeus is too obvious for comment; as is the general tone of dignity and high seriousness, leading to rhetorical flourishes and cadences without warrant in the original: 'toil, and sweat, and blood.' Rieu, on the contrary, is almost exaggeratedly concrete and unheroic. Pope's 'Jove' is 'The all-wise disposer of the fates of men'; Rieu's Zeus, 'too wary to be caught'. (The latter draws out a possible reading of the original; the former is without basis.) Rieu's Zeus clearly 'breaks[s] the twisted cord' of Teucer's bow as Homer describes; in Pope, the string is miraculously 'Struck by an arm unseen'. The heroic and fatal note in the exchange between Teucer and Ajax in Pope ('Some god prevents our destined enterprise', 'Thy arms no less suffice the lance to wield') is replaced in Rieu with wry, earthy colloquialism: 'Some evil power is spoiling everything', 'Well, my friend, you might as well ...'

The two versions relate divine and human, supernatural and natural, in radically different ways; so too with their depiction of the warrior's cast of mind, his speech and action in battle. They present the Homeric ethos and Homeric metaphysic in utterly different lights. It is clearly no accident that Pope's *Iliad* was composed in the shadow of Blenheim and Malplaquet, tinged by the more romantic adventurism of the Jacobite rebellion, the whole routed through the bookish militarism of a home-keeping neoclassical poet; while Rieu's appeared a few years after the

Second World War, in the strained milieu of late-1940s Britain, and was composed under the emphatically anti-elite ideology of the early days of the Penguin Classics.

Let us look at another contrast in lower key. Here are two versions of the opening of the Hellenistic Greek elegy by the pastoral poet Moschus for his predecessor Bion. The first is by J.M. Edmonds in the Loeb Classical Library, published in 1912:

Cry me waly upon him, you glades of the woods, and waly, sweet Dorian water; you rivers, weep I pray you for the lovely and delightful Bion. Lament you now, good orchards; gentle groves, make you your moan; be your breathing clusters, ye flowers, dishevelled for grief. Pray roses, now be your redness sorrow, and yours sorrow, windflowers; speak now thy writing, dear flower-de-luce, loud let thy blossoms babble ay; the beautiful musician is dead.[8]

And here is the 1975 Penguin Classics translation by Anthony Holden:

> Join, glades, my hymn of mourning;
> Dorian waters, lament with me;
> weep, rivers, weep for Bion, for his beauty.
> Now orchards, sorrow with me; sigh, groves;
> flowers, breathe grief from your tight clusters;
> now roses, deepen your red in mourning; and yours,
> anemones; now hyacinth, let your lettering speak,
> your leaves chatter their grief.
> The beautiful flute-player is dead.[9]

Even granted the fundamentally stylized nature of the source, Edmonds goes out of his way to ensure a particularly 'literary' translation. He adds further, incongruous frames of poetic convention, like that of the Scottish ballads. He introduces romantic-Victorian archaisms like 'ye' (of course); while 'windflowers', an apparently simple Saxon term, is actually an elite-classicist

equivalent of *anemone,* the English gardener's term retained by
Holden. Note also the heraldic 'flower-de-luce' for 'hyacinth', not
to mention the excruciating pun on *ay*—the markings on the
hyacinth were read as *ai,* the Greek expression of grief.

Holden's rendering, by contrast, is designedly direct and simple.
It operates at the inescapable basic level of poetry in an age of
more matter-of-fact (prosaic?) scholarship, most clearly seen in
rendering the line about the hyacinth's marking as 'Now, hyacinth,
let your lettering speak', which is meaningless to the uninformed
reader in the absence of a note. Holden also eschews any admixture
of poetic conventions from intervening ages or models. He is a
discreet purveyor or interpreter. Despite a loose underpinning of
verse form, his version seems to aim at a significational equivalent,
suggesting what the Greek conveyed while virtually implying that it
cannot be conveyed: as though following Ortega y Gasset's dictum
that 'the translation is not the work, but a path towards the work',
a kind of 'apparatus'.[10] Edmonds obviously saw himself as re-
creator: though he uses prose, he has made a bolder, if arguably
misguided, attempt at poetic equipollence.

For each passage, the two translations convey not merely the
different models of poetic utterance across decades or centuries,
but fundamentally different notions of verbal function and
equivalence, and of the relation between a classical Greek text,
contemporary 'home' culture, and intermediate literary convention.

Clearly, both renderings indicate the extension of Greek (or let
us for the time being, beg the question and say classical) culture
into later periods, but also the appropriation and transformation
of classical culture by the latter—indeed, considered over the span
of history, the continuous creation of the classical by each age in
its own image. The process is held to have started in the
Renaissance; but surely it is heralded by the medieval concept of

'the ancients', or indeed of the Roman cultivation of Hellenic models.

The basic process all through is the transformative assimilation of culture. Translation is one crucial expression of it. In fact, the entire assimilative process is a species of translation—or more truly, an expansion or magnification of translation. The translation of particular texts contributes to the 'translation' of a supposedly ancient discourse that is really the creation of a new discourse in terms drawn from one or more previous ones. The creation of 'the classical' consists in the prolonged assimilation of disparate ancient texts by bending and adapting them—translating them, often literally and certainly in a wider sense—to a unified discourse built up in a later age.

This translation-cum-absorption proceeds in concentric linguistic phases: Greek into Latin into Renaissance vernacular, and within this grossly simple model, chronological phases—Homeric to Hellenistic Greek, classical Latin through Medieval to Neo-Latin— as also social, dialectal and regional phases: Doric/Ionic/Aeolian, converging on a Greek lingua franca or *koine* as well as a more popular stratum; literary and Vulgar Latin, interacting and dispersing into the range of medieval latinities and reconverging in the Renaissance; and of course contributory patterns like the incursion of Arabic discourse in the European Middle Ages or the subliminal presence of Hebrew in the Renaissance. The multichronic, multilocational function of Latin is the most crucial factor in this model. To use a mathematical analogy, its place value differs constantly. It is now source now target language, and always a mediating linguistic presence; now it embodies the contemporary and now (or simultaneously) the 'timeless' ancient line. Its 'face value' too differs constantly: it is never the same Latin.

In translation, two ages and cultures—more strictly, two groups or conglomerates of culture—are held in tension, each reworked in the light of the other and further refracted by a range of other forces. We are finally left with the continually shifting interplay of amassed forces around two foci, the source and target cultures, focused in their turn upon two texts that are also one.

In this interaction and mutual appropriation, the host culture— i.e., that of the target language in the translator's age and milieu— apparently has the advantage of the last word. Clearly, the source text is being reworked in the light of the host culture. It vindicates Persse MacGarrigle, David Lodge's drunken researcher into the influence of T.S. Eliot on Shakespeare.[11] But equally, the source text is working upon the host language and culture, drawing out possibilities in the latter that would otherwise be unrealized. It is shaping the stuff of a living culture by the agency of a more or less remote and superseded text.

Philosophers from Foucault to Kuhn have accustomed us to the idea of sequence or continuity as disjuncture. It is an extension of the obvious view of evolution (as of course revolution) as disjuncture. In translation, the verbal transference carries its own disjunctive function, makes the translation something other than the original, reveals in the original the potential to be something other than itself. Even monolingual readings, and *a fortiori* translations and readings of translations (a single unfolding category: translations *are* readings, which then invite further non-scriptal readings), follow a trajectory of departures and innovations that redefine the 'original', the surface-bound, the intentionist.

The factor of intention is important; for it enables us to employ another paradigm of creative deviation, the 'anxiety of influence'. The translator, at least of the 'straight' category whose avowed purpose is to render the original in a new medium, might seem a species of textualizer singularly free from such anxiety: he is professing not merely influence but adherence. But Bloom's classic premiss of the anxiety of influence is simply an intentionist formulation of a process of linguistic dynamism whose roots lie in the resources of language and verbal form, in the impersonal fact of language's inevitable, literally infinite propensity to generate unique structures. By the very way words work, the 'influenced' poet must write differently from the 'influencing' one. The latter poet's intention can at most serve as one factor in this deviant, innovative role thrust upon him by his vocation of words.

Like the 'influenced' poet or 'imitator' (in the near-archaic sense to which I shall return), the translator makes explicit the re-creation of the text effected by each reader out of the bank or stock of significance invested in the text by the resources of the language and the total context of composition. What the translator additionally performs is to draw, as it were, upon the funds of another language-bank, set up a joint venture with another cultural corporation, thus obviously reducing the share of the original holder. Those who wish to play this market cannot but ask: who is buying up whom?

The answer will vary with circumstance. The equation is of one sort where source and host languages belong to the same cultural continuum—specially, but not necessarily, to the same language group as well. Where they are different, the equation falls into an utterly different category. A prime example of encounter across language families is, of course, between Hebrew and Hebraic on the one hand and the languages of Europe on the other, extending to other language-groups through the mediation of the European languages. The extent to which these host languages and cultures have been reshaped by Semitic influence is quite immeasurable, to a point where the very distinction of the two seems untenable.

More seismic, because more compressed in time and dramatically extended in area, is the encounter of the colonizing languages and cultures of Europe and the greater part of the world's other cultures, widening out at the present time into an Anglophone hegemony that is at the same time revolutionizing the English language and Anglophone cultures across the world.

Only one degree less marked is the encounter of different groups within the same family: the epic encounter of Greek and Latin in Europe for two thousand years and more (again moderated through the modern European languages into other languages and cultures); or, less only by comparison, the primacy of Italian as the lead factor in the interplay of European vernaculars in the Renaissance (I have spoken already of the relations between the vernaculars, classical Latin and Neo-Latin); or the hegemony of French in a more recent period in Europe, leading on to the chiasmic pattern of interaction between French and English, the authority of the former gradually yielding to the latter between the eighteenth and the twentieth centuries. There are fascinating socio-linguistic implications to the snatches of French in *Anna Karenina* or, more extensively, *The Magic Mountain.* (They are, of course, utterly different from such incursions in earlier texts, like the French scene in Shakespeare's *Henry V.*)

Derrida has drawn our attention to 'the possibility for languages to be implicated *more than two* in a text'.[12] The ultimate instance of such counterpollence of languages, moderating the semiotic scope of each by that of others, lies in the 'macaronic' poems typically known from the European Middle Ages but found in other ages and cultures as well.

> Cette est ma volunté
> That I might be with thee,
> Ludendo.

Votre amour en mon coeur
Brenneth hot as doth the fire,
Crescendo.[13]

There is no direct translation here—indeed, the point of the poem is that there is not—but in another perspective, each line is a putative 'translation' of the implicit equivalent in any or all of the other languages being used. Each line is supplemented, each line is subverted, by these suggested presences behind the text.

All intrusions of a second language in the original text, all passages standing out in relief, represent a significant phenomenon of non-translation in the discourse of the original. They are rightly left untranslated in translations of the original—as traditionally with the French passages in Tolstoy and Mann. But what will a French translator do? The obverse problem arose in a recent anthology of translations from modern Bengali poetry that I helped to edit.[14] Like other Indian languages, modern Bengali, specially in its spoken and informal registers, is strongly interlarded with English words, even where there are perfectly good Bengali equivalents that would be used in formal contexts. In an English rendering, the only course seemed to be to italicize these words, with a note to the reader explaining the practice. (The same device was earlier adopted by Gayatri Chakravorty Spivak in translating from Mahasweta Devi.[15]) But a printing convention like this makes for a signpost, not an integrated utterance. In the new (English) verbal milieu of the translation, the English words acquire a different relation to their context, perform a different function. We might render, quite literally, the letter of the original, but not the cultural interface on which it was located.

Any translation of a particular text must be plotted against the play of cultural politics. A translation from one language to another reflects the balance of relationships between them, that is to say their user-groups, but at the same time subtly modifies that balance. A Renaissance translation from Italian into English would indicate a direction of influence, a particular slant of reception, contrary to a hypothetical translation from English into Italian. Significantly, it must be hypothetical: there were no such translations in the Renaissance. The only notable work of English origin to be rendered in any other language in the Renaissance was More's *Utopia,* into French; and significantly again, the source text was in Latin, at a different level in the hierarchy of languages. (Of course, it was also translated into English.) All this contrasts sharply with the current position in cross-translations between English and Italian. Specially in the case of non-European originals, translations are frequently made out of those languages through English into Italian. Of the 28 published volumes of Italian versions of Rabindranath Thakur (Tagore), only one might have been rendered directly from the Bengali.[16]

Another category of cultural encounter mediated by translation is between two groups *within* the target culture. In Britain in the later nineteenth century, there was an immense range of English translations from the classics and from other European languages. They were aimed at the beneficiaries of the growing network of continuing and informal education, the designedly limited second-best systems aimed at women and working-class men outside the clientele of the classically-oriented university. Ultimately, these translations catered to the autodidacts fostered by such a milieu.

But if the milieu encouraged them, it also 'placed' them in their socially determined echelon. It enlightened them and deprived them, liberated them and confined them. The subscriber to Bohn's Classical Library was struggling for a foothold in the world of the classically-trained elite. The translation, for such a user, confirmed the gap in the very process of bridging it. By the fact of using a translation, he was excluded from the world of his classicist compatriot. Today's British reader of the Penguin Classics might be left as remote from the original Greek or Latin; but in a non-classicist intellectual milieu, what matters is not the fundamental remoteness but the secondary understanding, the obvious and unabashed adaptation of orthodox classicist discourse to a culture-system regulated by the mother tongue.

Granted this wide range of variation in cultural encounters through translation, we may define it in terms of three intersecting principles: a synchronic, contemporary, overtly political equation, countered to varying extent by diachronic, historical factors, and/ or by supposedly non-contingent intellectual or aesthetic criteria. A translation out of modern Greek into English embodies a different balance of these factors from one out of classical Greek; the balance would have been sharply more contrastive in the nineteenth century. To this day, the literatures of east European countries, with the notable exception of Russia, complain of critical neglect by the West-dominated literary establishment.

The Dutch writer Cees Nooteboom lamented recently in the *Washington Post Book World* that 'a small country, whose literature is written in a secret code, is, to a certain extent, non-existent.'[17] Needless to say, such effacement is owing to (and measured by) the lack of translations, while the lack of translations is owing to the effacement. The translation scenario between two languages or cultures 'fixes' or crystallizes their hegemonic relationship. Hence Bernard Cohn can use translation as a trope for the cultural encounter, and attempted expropriation, of Indian culture by the British in colonial times:

The production of these texts [i.e., studies of Indian languages and translations from them] began the establishment of discursive formation,

defined an epistemological space, created a disourse (Orientalism), and
had the effect of converting Indian forms of knowledge into European
objects. ... The languages that the Indians speak and read were to be
transformed. The discursive formation was to participate in the creation
and reification of social groups with their varied interests. It was to establish
and regularize a discourse of differentiations that came to mark the social
and political map of nineteenth-century India.[18]

Yet by articulating the hegemony, each translation from a
marginal or subaltern language into a dominant one can counter
the imbalance—often subtly, sometimes dramatically. It validates
the subaltern culture quite literally in terms of the dominant one;
but thereby draws out the dominant language beyond its
entrenched confines.

In Homi K. Bhabha's words, 'Cultural translation is not simply
appropriation or adaptation; it is a process through which cultures
are required to revise their own systems and values, by departing
from their habitual or "inbred" rules of transformation.
Ambivalence and antagonism accompany any act of cultural
translation, because negotiating with the "difference of the other"
reveals the radical insufficiency of our own systems of meaning
and signification.'[19] Aniket Jaaware describes the process more
elaborately:

One has to de-spirit one's own language first, one has to dispossess
oneself of the spirit of one's own language, and then re-inspire the
benumbed body with another spirit. ... The own-ness of one's own world
is distanced in translation. Entirely to be dispossessed of one's world —
such is the risk in translation. There is always the possibility that one's
own benumbed body may fail to house a stranger spirit ... But there is
risk also in the rising of the body with a stranger spirit. This body can
move about only awkwardly, strangely, somewhat inhumanly.[20]

We have here another perspective on the ambivalent cultural

encounter implicit in the act of translation.

Nonetheless, the ambivalence of such ambivalence, the improbability of the metempsychosis postulated by Jaaware, is strikingly exemplified in the reception of Rabindranath Thakur's own English versions of his Bengali poems in *Gitanjali (Song-Offerings)*, which led to the award of the Nobel Prize in 1913. Undoubtedly, part of Rabindranath's appeal to the Western reader of the day was the poetic, exotic cast of his language. It corresponded to an orientalist exoticism cultivated by English poets for over a century by that date, from Moore and Southey through Edwin Arnold to James Elroy Flecker; but this, as it were, was the real thing, straight out of the east. Yet beyond this confirmation of a trend in English poetic language, there was the decisive factor of colonial patronage, the certification of a subaltern culture in terms not its own and therefore leaving the field open for its subsequent dismissal by the dominant culture when the latter acquired new tastes and made new demands of poetry. The dismissal was made easier by a spate of hasty and indifferent renderings that followed the *Gitanjali* volume to cater to the demand of the moment.

The history of the reception of Rabindranath's translations of his own work reveals the fundamental helplessness of a translator projecting a subaltern culture in a hegemonic situation, the limited and self-defeating nature of any rehabilitation of that culture by such means. The receiving culture becomes in effect the controlling and assessing power. The host admits the guest very much on his own terms: overtly in Rabindranath's case, covertly and paradoxically where the absorption appears so deep as to become organic to the host milieu, the autonomy of the original irrecoverably lost. A good instance of this would be Fitzgerald's version of Omar Khayyam. The Persian poet is yanked out of his times and context to participate in a Victorian counterculture.

In its orientalist guise, this counterculture was of course merely a version of the dominant imperial culture of the age. 'It is an amusement to me,' wrote Fitzgerald in a now notorious letter, 'to take what liberties I like with these Persians, who ... really do want a little Art to shape them.'[21] In the broadest sense, all such hegemonies are colonial or imperial: often, of course, literally so, as in Rabindranath's case. The colonial equation might not be a simple one. The line of political, military or economic colonization might apparently be countered by the cultural hegemony. The readiest example is the cultural precedence granted to ancient Greece by its Roman conquerors, as expressed in the historian's cliché that Greece conquered Rome culturally even while Rome was conquering Greece militarily. Such clichés obscure the balancing reality of cultural appropriation—the sense of fulfilling what lesser predecessors had begun, of finding brick and leaving marble. We may compare the spirit in which Christian humanists in the Renaissance commandeered the substance of ancient pagan culture. This is another crucial aspect of the cultural translation underlying and underscoring the endemic lingual translations of that age. In medieval Latin, a crucial implication of *translatio* was the cultural movement from Greece to Rome to Paris, a *translatio studii* (transfer of learning) running *pari passu* with the *translatio imperii* (transfer of rule) whereby Charlemagne's rule was vested with the authority of the Roman empire.[22]

In contrast to ancient Rome, modern colonialism offers a new phenomenon. No longer is there a two-way tension between political and cultural hegemonies. Instead, a two-way translation traffic (not found in any earlier period) conceals the unidirectional flow of cultural power and control. Not only are the texts of the dominant, colonizing culture translated into those of the colonized community, there is also a substantial reverse flow—not as at the

Graeco-Roman change of guard, where Greek models were valued, sustained and absorbed by the Romans, but now as the instrument of cultural subordination, frequently masked by an aloof spirit of detached scholarship or curiosity. Such translations are undertaken in the spirit of, and often as an actual component of, historical, sociological and anthropological studies, with the cultural and political control implicit in such pursuits. Such is the textualizing of the East that Said marked long ago as a fundamental feature of Orientalism.[23]

Nineteenth-century Europe saw an unprecedented surge of translations from the languages of colonized cultures. This fact must be recognized, even if (as claimed and statistically borne out),[24] the total quantum of translations into English declined sharply in this period. The new class of translations contained a ballast of hard-core scholarship, sometimes unsurpassed to this day; they could reach awesome heights of intellectual or even physical adventure. This intellectual involvement surely led at times to genuine absorption of and respect for the material of these alien cultures—even, rarely, a marked idealization, as of ancient Indian culture by certain European Sanskritists. But the body of such translations, with their ancillary scholarship and pseudo-scholarship, patently aims to project alien cultures, credited with sharply restricted value, on the lower rungs of a hegemony of civilizations determined by the colonial order itself.

Yet only through such translations could the colonized or underling community, the cultural subaltern, at all find recognition from the dominant or ruling power. Its colours were apparent to the imperial eye only when it was pinned and wriggling on the wall. Hence the representation, even the distortion of its culture in an uncongenial medium became a matter of value, and sometimes of pride, to the colonized nation—also at times a matter of practical necessity, especially in a multilingual region like South Asia, where such translations provided (and distressingly often, still provide) the only text possessed in common by scholars of various language-groups. To this day, the Indian scholar of his own culture is heavily reliant on, and conditioned by, translations and interpretations not only in English but often by Western, specially Anglophone scholars. He may designedly confine himself to the tools and resources of Anglophone academia. He persists in seeing his own culture through imported spectacles.

The tendency is not new: and as I said before, it is inevitable, given the wealth of material and seminal paradigms afforded by colonial means. Tod's *Annals and Antiquities of Rajasthan,* for instance, compiled the lore of a dramatic and colourful period of western Indian history as no Indian agency has done before or since. Hence with all its imperial as well as feudal-chivalric preconceptions, exacerbated by whatever defects of transmission and linguistic inadequacy, the book mediated an Indian discovery of India's own heritage. It was notably used by Rabindranath (and his nephew Abanindranath) to create a body of patriotic myth directed specially towards children and youth in the formative period of India's freedom movement.

The process can be rewritten as farce. In 1883 the Reverend Lal Behary Dey, an Indian Christian convert and missionary, wrote *Folk Tales of Bengal,* at the suggestion of an English army captain, as a declared contribution to the international literature of folklore and comparative mythology. As late as 1977, a noted Bengali writer, Lila Majumdar, translated Dey's book into Bengali to be read by Bengali children! The implied play of hegemonic forces is fascinating.

A crucial dimension of the colonial encounter-through-translation lies not in the direct commerce between colonizer and colonized, but its reflection in intra-communal disparities in the colonized or post-colonial society. One effect provides an interesting parallel to the encounter of classicist and non-classicist social groups in nineteenth-century England. In India, the Indian languages have produced a range of translations from English (sometimes from other European languages through English, seldom directly from another European language); the consumers of these are the sections of society not trained, or not adequately trained, in English, who would still be regarded in most Indian situations as educationally and socially disadvantaged (even if, sometimes today, politically privileged). The Indian elite would read such works in English. Interestingly, they might even read Sanskrit works, or those from other Indian languages, in English rendering, even where there are translations in Indian languages they can access.

Again, in such societies, going by the example of India, translations from the local language into English attract close attention and comment, often far exceeding their reception among the target Anglophone readership. In particular, an English translation of Rabindranath's work becomes a notable cultural event among the very Bengalis who need take no interest in it. The most extensive publicity, as well as the most long-drawn and acrimonious controversies about Rabindranath in recent years have centred not on his Bengali texts or Bengali studies of them but on certain English renderings.

The motive emerges clearly from the terms of all such discussion. These translations are seen as presenting Rabindranath, hence Bengali and Indian culture and civilization, to the world. A culture that regards itself as intrinsically 'major', but that is marginalized partly by restrictions of language and partly by long-standing colonial subordination, is looking for its due place in the quasi-colonial world cultural hegemony. Hence each translation by a native Bengali is seen as a strategy of cultural marketing; by an Anglophone translator as a registered sale. Colonially-conditioned contexts of reception can place more value on such extrinsic recognition than on intrinsic merit. Rabindranath himself was convinced that his winning the Nobel Prize materially affected the light in which his countrymen regarded his work. He has been charged with evincing something of the same syndrome in his own programme of translation. It is magnified in the politics surrounding present-day translations of his work and, to a lesser extent, those of other Indian writers.

While by this view, translations are presented as attempts to break the cultural hierarchy, they serve collaterally if not primarily to perpetuate it. Each such presentation confirms the hegemony of reception. Whatever the professed terms of presentation, the translated poet from across the line is shown up as a species of interloper in a cultural system defined in other terms and contexts.

There are times when the encounter of two cultures through translation resembles nothing so much as the encounter of two strange dogs sniffing and circling each other. Translation, the ground and medium of cultural exchange, is organically invested with destabilizing and distancing factors. This is the full, perturbing implication of the glib premiss that no translation is culturally neutral.

2

The Translator
as Sceptic

Perhaps more than any other intellectual endeavour, translation rests on a basic defeatism of outlook. Whatever other purposes a translation might serve, whatever new creative energies it might unleash, as a translation or rendering it must always be inadequate, never a total reflection or equivalent of the original. There is no synonymity between languages or indeed within a language. Translation attempts the futile task of making two unique verbal entities coincide: it is like those *trompes de l'oeuil* which make two dissimilar shapes appear to resemble each other.

I obtained unusual confirmation of this truism while translating into English the nonsense-verse of the classic Bengali children's writer, Sukumar Ray.[25] Nonsense verse might be regarded as the type of writing most difficult to translate, as even approximate correspondence is out of the question—not only with actual nonsense-words and coinages, but with the exceptionally incongruous mix of culture-specific ingredients. In fact, however, I found that this avowed impossibility had a liberating effect. Freed from the fiction of equivalence, the mismatch between source and output became a declared factor in the exercise. Nonsense writing, by definition, does not convey a fixed sober version of reality that asks futilely to be preserved.

The translator of 'serious' poetry has a more difficult task. Unlike nonsense verse, serious poetry does not deny its own final validity, but the mere fact of translation implies such a denial—just as translation challenges the assurance of meaning assumed in quotidian unreflective utterance. It points out that such meaning is not absolute, but convertible to something other than itself. It reminds us that language cannot enshrine any 'truth', any objective *signifié*. 'Truth' inheres in arbitrary combinations of signs and sounds. Translation provides the readiest confirmation of the basic principles of Saussurean semantics. 'Whether we try,' says Saussure,

to find the meaning of the Latin word *arbor* or the word that Latin uses to designate the concept "tree", it is clear that only the associations sanctioned by that language appear to us to conform to reality, and we disregard whatever others might be imagined.[26]

Translation, then, is the philosophically redoubtable project of transferring a 'reality' from its native verbal habitat to another: or to put it another way, extending a 'reality' beyond its proper verbal confines, formulating it in terms other than the original ones in which it was experienced and defined—which are, strictly, the only ones in which it can be valid. One is led towards the image of an organ transplant whose viability is constantly in question.

It is a philosophic problem, but it is also central to the politics of translation, subtilizing the issue beyond the point I reached in my last chapter. Because all translations are imperfect matches, the components of a translated culture rank lower in an epistemological hierarchy than the elements of the host culture. Simply put, the cultural material 'native' to a language naturally appears more viable, hence more valuable, than material translated into that language out of some other culture. When we hear a foreigner talking our language imperfectly, we vulgarly conclude that the man is dim-witted, that his very understanding of things is inferior to ours. Something analogous happens when we comprehend an author in translation: he is speaking another tongue, trying to make himself understood in a language not his own. His premisses are that much less likely to seem valid. 'We shouldn't be surprised that a translated author always seems somewhat foolish to us,' says Ortega y Gasset bluntly.[27]

Hence at times, the epistemological hierarchy can counter the socio-political one. In imperial times, the 'translation' of the British colonialists' culture could pass from the usual exemplary mode into the parodic or ironic through literal rendering into the language or milieu of the ruled. Writing a satirical 'Hymn to the Englishman' in 1872 (whose target is the obsequious Babu offering worship, rather than the sahib receiving it), Bankimchandra Chattopadhyay translates the attributes of the Englishman into those of the Hindu gods. (The italicized words were embedded in English form in the Bengali text, reinforcing the pastiche otherwise effected by the translation itself.)

You are Indra, the cannon is your thunder; you are Chandra the moon-god, the income tax is your stain; you are Vayu the wind-god, the railway is your passage; you are Varuna the sea-god, the sea is your kingdom. Hence, O Englishman, I bow to you...

You are without doubt the Krishna of our age. The hat is your cowherd's headgear, trousers your garb, the whip your enchanting flute. Hence, O beloved of milkmaids, I bow to you. ...

Invite me to your *dinners* and *at-homes;* make me a *member* of great *committees,* a *member* of the *senate,* a *justice,* an *honorary magistrate:* I bow to you.

Hear my *speeches,* read my *essays,* applaud me—I shall not heed the strictures of all Hindu society. I bow to you alone.[28]

The first part 'translates' not words but features and attributes to bring out the enormity of the cultural mismatch. In the second part, the strategy is reversed: English words are set in the Bengali text to convey the alien nature of the institutions and practices described.

In 1928, Rajshekhar Basu, under the pen-name of Parashuram, wrote a historical fantasy 'Ulat-Puran', 'The Scripture Read Backward',[29] where India is imagined to have conquered Britain and Europe. One aspect of the cultural domination is the appropriation and distortion of European place-names as the British distorted Indian ones: following common Indian structures, the Mediterranean Sea becomes 'Metipukur', Ulster 'Belestara', Switzerland 'Chhachhurabad'. The phonic and sememic implications are reductive in each case. But no less reductive is the literal rendering of common English idioms—'loaves and fishes', 'land flowing with milk and honey'—in the pamphlets of British freedom-fighters. Translated into Bengali, they acquire an outré, unserious touch.

'Ulat-Puran' is a wish-fulfilling fantasy. Colonial positions are realistically portrayed in the short story 'Swayambara',[30] where a devout Brahmin plays the improbable priest at a marriage between two American tourists on an Indian train. Rajshekhar creates a remarkable vividness and authenticity of tone by retaining a few English words in his Bengali rendering of the Americans' speech; simultaneously, he frames the whole within the subaltern perspective by introducing Indian terms and images. The bride's face is a Chinese berry; her painted lips two ripe chillis; the old Brahmin's blessing upon her is 'May the vermillion on your lips never fade.' The parodic function of translation operates pervasively and insidiously in translations from subaltern to dominant language.

The common assumption of the objective validity of language, of a reality 'out there' to which our words refer and correspond, extends by suggestion even to planes where we grant that the reality-principle cannot apply: to ideas, systems and values. These are validated in terms of a particular verbal system, and that validation implies an assumed tenability, an actuality or 'truth'. Translation, then, appears to posit an impossibility: degrees of 'truth', objectivity or absoluteness—which are, of course, actually degrees of value by some particular system of gradation. To translate something is to assess it in terms of another culture, another language-system that is simultaneously another value-system, and thus inevitably find it wanting. It is held to be Caliban's fault, not Prospero's, that Prospero does not understand Caliban's language; the latter can be redeemed only when his sense is commuted into Prospero's tongue by a Procrustean exercise:

> When thou didst not, savage,
> Know thine own meaning, but wouldst gabble like
> A thing most brutish, I endow'd thy purposes
> With words that made them known.[31]

Lexical comprehension does not eliminate the gabble-hunting syndrome. One might understand a text in and through translation, but still not imbibe it. With an unquestionably remote text, such as Hittite or Akkadian, scholars admit to being confined to such a mechanical, external understanding. As one such scholar, N.K. Sandars, has said, 'The meaning when arrived at is still an archaeological object which has to be articulated into life.'[32]

The readiest means by which translators attempt to counter such devaluation of the source-language is by annotational rendering. The translation is invested with an explanatory dimension that the original did not have. Here is the opening of 'The Patriot', Rabindranath's own translation of his Bengali short story 'Samskara'. I have italicized the sections for which there is no corresponding text in the original:

I am sure that Chitragupta, *who keeps strict record at the gate of Death,* must have noted down in big letters accusations against me, which had escaped my attention altogether. ...

My wife's name [Kalika] *means literally a 'bud'.* It was given by my father-in-law, who is thus solely responsible for any discrepancy [from] the reality to which it is attached. ... Once, when she had been vigorously engaged in picketing against British cloth in Burrabazar, the awe-struck members of her party ... gave her the name 'Dhruva-vrata', *the woman of unwavering vows.*

My name is Girindra, *the Lord of the Rocks, so common among my countrymen, whose character generally fails to act up to it.*[33]

That last expansion is on a different plane: it does not merely define the literal meaning but explains the ironic implication, which is by no means obvious in the original.

'Annotational' rendering can take various forms. A notable 'hidden' version is the expansion of implied grammatical structures —which can allegedly amount to *imposing* syntax and structure—in compressed old Chinese texts whose syntax is not amenable to Indo-European patterns nor, apparently, to modern Chinese ones. Arthur Waley has been specially charged with such attempts at elucidation, which his successors have sometimes seen as restrictive.[34] We must reflect that precisely the same problem has been noted in translating the staccato jottings that make up the Greek text of Aristotle's *Poetics*, like many other of his works: hence, in Gilbert Murray's phrase, 'the long series of misunderstandings and overstatements and corrections which form the history of the Poetics since the Renaissance'.[35]

A stage beyond 'annotational translation' lies formal annotation, an apparatus beyond the translated text. 'I want translations with copious footnotes, footnotes reaching up like skyscrapers,' declared Nabokov.[36] But the distancing effect of such a practice militates against the literal comprehension it affords: the translated culture is conclusively fenced-off, made other, the subject of a sustained critique beyond the limits of the translation itself. This can have a reorienting effect on members of the native culture if they encounter the translated texts—as often with colonial or postcolonial cultures accessing their own material through Western studies and translations. The resulting detachment can have a range of outcomes, from enhanced understanding to discontent and reform or, of course, hostile rejection of the implicit critique. The last reaction grants by its very rejection the potency of a variant perspective, a new angle on the material, a view of themselves as others see them.

By offering such perspectives, translation provides an obvious tool in the programme of the Sceptic. In vulgar use, it can cater to scepticism in the vulgar sense, dismissing other systems from the supposedly absolute vantage-ground of one's own target-language and culture—in other words, an exercise the very reverse of the truly Sceptical. The source text is placed in an alien semiotic frame which is at the same time the reader's accustomed and natural frame. It is thereby rightly exposed as contingent, relative, arbitrary in import, its substance not truly substantial; but the host language and culture function as putative absolutes.

By a rarer exercise of the epistemology of translation, we arrive at a truly Sceptical sense of the relative nature of all premises, all discourse, all texts and verbal systems. As the prince of Renaissance Sceptics puts it,

Our speech has its weaknesses and its defects, like all the rest. Most of the occasions for the troubles of the world are grammatical. Our lawsuits spring only from debate over the interpretation of the laws, and most of our wars from the inability to express clearly the conventions and treaties of agreement of princes. How many quarrels, and how important, have been produced in the world by doubt of the meaning of that syllable *Hoc!* ...

I can see why the Pyrrhonian philosophers cannot express their general conception in any manner of speaking; for they would need a new language.[37]

Now the interesting thing about a full-fledged Sceptical programme is that it passes beyond subversion and dismissal into a position of open-minded acceptance. Scepticism can induce a willing suspension of disbelief in *all* texts, hence an openness to all cultural and intellectual positions. This can be coupled with a declaredly pragmatic, contingent adherence to the particular system of one's own native culture: in his social stance, the Sceptic is often an entrenched conservative. 'The wise man,' says Montaigne, 'should withdraw his soul within, out of the crowd, and keep it in power and freedom to judge things freely; but as for externals, he should wholly follow the accepted fashions and forms. ... For it is the rule of rules, and the universal law of laws, that each man should observe those of the place he is in.'[38] But that last sentence provides the balancing factor. The Sceptic allows the same privilege to people of all cultures, and thus prepares the ground for interaction on a non-hierarchic footing.

I do not share that common error of judging another by myself. I easily believe that another man may have qualities different from mine. Because I feel myself tied down to one form, I do not oblige everybody to espouse it, as all others do. I believe in and conceive a thousand contrary ways of life.[39]

By implication, the Sceptic goes farther still, thereby undermining his own premises in a way even a Sceptic might not intend. Interaction, albeit among disparate entities, argues interrelation, a common ground between disjunct minds, systems and cultures. Montaigne's view of cannibals presents them as being nearer the primal source of a continuum of the human state. They

retain alive and vigorous their genuine, their most useful and natural, virtues and properties, which we have debased in the latter in adapting them to gratify our corrupted taste. ... It is not reasonable that art should win the place of honour over our great and powerful mother Nature. We have so overloaded the beauty and richness of her works by our inventions that we have quite smothered her.[40]

'Here's three on's are sophisticated! Thou art the thing itself.'[41] 'The thing itself', the 'natural' state, postulates an essentiality, of language as of the beings who employ language. It argues at very least for an underlying correspondence between all sign-systems that, among innumerable other consequences, alone makes the translator's task conceivable, makes it indeed a familiar working reality.

I am reassembling the pieces left by the deconstructive argument of my first chapter. I am stressing the familiar and positive side of the ambivalence that I had earlier treated in more subversive spirit. The translator looks at his source and finds a text that has already arranged itself in a manner compatible or overlapping with the structures of the target language, a guest that shares with his host certain basic conventions of etiquette and discourse. A quantum of signification can, it seems, be transferred from one verbal system to another without thought to their respective surface structures or the precise forms of the original and translated texts.

This naive point—which, after all, underlies the making and reading of all translations—is readily illustrated from the prose renderings of poetic texts: in prose, it seems, precisely because of the translator's deep awareness of the inimitable poetic qualities of the original. Robert Durling provides an apologia for his translations of *Petrarch's Lyric Poems:*

... it is because the formal elaboration of the *Rime sparse* is both so integral to their greatness and so problematic that I have chosen prose. I hope the absence of rhyme will continually remind the reader to look across at the Italian. My translation is meant to be a guide to the original, not an equivalent.

Yet with surprising directness for a work published in 1976, and begging immense questions of language and poetic form, he claims for his exercise a positive function: 'a literal prose translation can at least convey the sense straightforwardly and show that much of Petrarch's interest as a poet does reside in the sense.'[42] This is bluntly, even naively put; but it points to a tenable principle of rendering. The very absence of formal correspondence highlights the basic transaction, and the principle of transaction, between two verbal orders.

Here, if anywhere, we find an essentialism implicit in the process of translation. It is of course a ready concomitant of all exercises in comparative literature and comparative linguistics, of which translation clearly constitutes a major branch. Few comparativists today might directly echo Charles Mills Gayley's view of literature as 'irrespective of age and guise, prompted by the common needs and aspirations of man, sprung from common faculties, and ... obeying common laws of material and mode, of the individual and social humanity.'[43] But it is unnecessary to profess such a universalism of ideology. The comparativist's method and purpose both imply a fundamental affinity of substance—'kinship' rather than 'likeness', in Walter Benjamin's terms.[44]

We may not follow Benjamin into his premiss of a 'pure language' (*reine Sprache*) where the imperfect postulates of actual languages supplement each other. But even at its most contrastive and phenomenally-oriented, comparativist study must postulate comparable and relatable categories running through its disparate material. As Umberto Eco very sensibly says, there is an assumption of the translatability of natural languages, underlying any concept of a universal artificial language, any communication between nations. Incommensurable structures can be compared and mutually rendered in terms of a common 'interpretative principle' not itself a language.[45] Translation puts this affinity or comparability in the sharpest possible focus by bringing two languages into unmediated contact, without the diversion or intervention of commentary—which must necessarily be in only one of the two languages or neither.

Relativism and essentialism are the two obverse, equal articles of the translator's faith. The attempt to relate them runs as the central motif through that classic, humane, meticulously argued and uniquely documented study of 'Aspects of Language and Translation', George Steiner's *After Babel*.[46] It is hard to say anything about translation that has not been anticipated somewhere in Steiner's work, to take up a position that he has not allowed for and incorporated into his scheme. But by my reading, through all Steiner's conscientious weighing of relativist and absolutist schools against each other, he is finally falling back—or longing to fall back—on an absolutist (shall I say ecumenical?) position, some profound level of deep structure or even some unexpressed, internalized, ur-stuff of utterance. In the simpler context of his introduction to the collection *Poem into Poem,* Steiner talks explicitly of a presumed 'third language' that intervenes in translation, 'a medium of communicative energy which somehow reconciles both languages in a tongue deeper, more comprehensive than either.'[47] This recalls Walter Benjamin's premiss quoted a short while ago.

Despite apparent divergence, the pattern is essentially repeated on the plane of formal philosophy in Andrew Benjamin's thoughtful study, *Translation and the Nature of Philosophy*. Benjamin examines and dismisses a number of views that argue for a unitary, objectivist or essentialist view of language. But his own scheme, designed to eliminate distinctions between 'inside' and 'outside', 'loss' and 'recovery', ultimately sites all variation in a text that constitutes a 'word', an originating or converging point of 'differential plurality'.[48]

Let us assume that there is such a level where all the waters of language meet. It is of little consequence to children paddling by the shore or gathering pebbles, which represents the linguistic situation of most users of words. The common ground between languages, their correspondence as regards some profound functions, is an inescapable 'given' in all acts of translation. Their profound differences are often left unprobed, though their superficial lexical mismatch is of course a commonplace of discussion. Alberto Manguel links the sense of commonality and shared significance with the sense of disjuncture and otherness in the carefully negative phrasing of his own postulation:

Translation proposes a sort of parallel universe [to that of the original work], another space and time in which the text reveals other, extraordinary possible meanings. For these meanings, however, there are no words, since they exist in the intuitive no man's land between the language of the original and the language of the translator.[49]

Taking off from these divergent but relatable positions, I am proposing a view of translation, and a process of translation, that actively fosters the relativist standpoint, that sees in a translated text a locus of contact between two otherwise floating, disparate, contingent structures of culture and communication; a view that regards source-text and output-text as binaries encircling one another, neither of them a static body. I am proposing that the usual politics of translation as outlined in my first chapter should be turned inside out. I am basing myself on the radically contingent dimension of all verbal exercises, precluding any set politics of translation. I am proposing that the metaphysics of translation be given a humane and practical application.

To propose such a stand on the theoretical plane is one thing; to lay out strategies for its practice, quite another. The readiest is obviously through certain modified forms of translation—so-called imitations, adaptations and the like, which allow for a change of context as well as language. I shall deal with these later on. I shall argue that such adaptations constitute a graded process of reception, a varied and extensive interface between cultures, across which the cultural traffic and indeed the intellectual activity of the world is carried out.

The 'straight' translation affords the least ready and obvious ground for two-way traffic, and it is difficult to lay down principles. The basic aim, of course, must be to displace or destabilize the hegemonically dominant language—which can be either source or target language, as I tried to demonstrate in my first chapter.

This is easier to conceive in terms of a publishing programme or choice of titles, rather than the intrinsic process of translation. Clearly, the expansion of translation lists by international publishers marks one significant step in the equalization of cultures: in particular the greater inclusion of titles from non-Western languages in the *literary* lists of Western publishers—i.e., titles chosen overtly for their intrinsic verbal or formal qualities, not for motives of antiquarian or area study. But this is only the most preliminary requirement: the crucial factor must be the conditions of conversion, the balance of cultures within the translated text. And here, as I have argued, we are still caught within the international cultural hegemony, which closely reflects the political and economic hegemony.

Not all translation scenarios are hegemonic. They can be non-interactive, non-relational. A curious situation obtains in translations between various Indian languages. (I have alluded to the matter earlier in a different perspective.) In a multilingual country with flourishing literatures in at least a dozen languages, there is singularly little translation between them (and that little unevenly distributed, owing to social and historical circumstances that might be hegemonic in nature). A reader of one Indian language can often read a work in another, if at all, only through English translation. For a nation with an intensely interactive federal life, Indian literatures operate to an improbable extent in conditions of exclusivity, linked chiefly by a certain classical and more proximate colonial legacy, and for the rest by non-verbal factors like social and religious practice and political inheritance. In such a situation, the absolutism of each language within its territory can be near-total, though of course it varies from case to case. I shall deal later with more aspects of India's multilingualism. It affords a number of possibly unique case-studies of the issues I am concerned with.

But what of an open view of language and culture *within* the translation, of working into the translated text a metalingual sense of the contingent and relative nature of both source and target languages, as of both the mediated cultures? At this point, the theorist of translation might feel he has bitten off more than he can chew. Prescriptions are difficult, and sound feeble when made. A sense of linguistic openness might be conveyed by the approximate prose translation, that devalues the precise form of the original by eschewing any compulsion to imitate it (even though the professed motive might be high valuation of the source text, a sense of its uniqueness). Equally, it might be conveyed by a formally exact rendering that implicitly denies the putative uniqueness of the original.

One means can be the penetration of the target language by the source language. The restructuring or contextualizing of one syntax and vocabulary, hence one culture-system, by another offers obvious testimony to the relative and fluid nature of both. Rudolf Pannitz's comments are relevant here:

Our translations, even the best, proceed from a false premise. They want to germanize Hindi, Greek, English, instead of hindi-izing, graecizing, anglicizing German. ... The fundamental error of the translator is that he maintains the accidental state of his own language, instead of letting it suffer the shock of the foreign language. ... [H]e must widen and deepen his language through the foreign one.[50]

Such penetration of the source language into the host language is a new feature of radical implications in post-war, post-colonial translation.

In William Radice's translation of Rabindranath's 'Sagarika' ('Sea-Maiden'), first published in 1985, the hero retains his *makara*-crested crown from the original. (The *makara* is a mythical sea beast.) When the woman by the sea is startled at his approach, he reassures her:

> 'Do not be afraid.
> I have come to pick puja-offerings in your flowering wood.'[51]

I have designedly chosen a native English translator, to draw more sharply the contrast with an Indian, Humayun Kabir, a notable patriot and political leader. Kabir's version was published in 1966, but written in the idiom of an earlier age. Kabir rendered the phrases in question as a 'dragon crown' and 'I only want to gather from your garden flowers for my God.'[52] The latter rendering is specially misleading, for this puja or worship is clearly offered as much or more to the woman. Perhaps Kabir was aiming at a clichéd 'Indian spirituality'; but his idiom and diction are strikingly different from the Englishman's twenty years later.

Another example from Radice is still more telling. In the poem 'Dui Bigha Jami' ('A Half-Acre of Land'), the speaker, a poor peasant, is robbed of his land by the landlord. He becomes a wandering ascetic. On his return to his village years later, the landlord charges him with stealing two mangoes from what was once his own tree.

> I said, 'Two mangoes are all I beg of you, master.'
> He sneered, 'He dresses as a *sadhu* but he's a pukka robber.'
> I wept, but I laughed as well at the irony of life—
> For he was now the great *sadhu*, and I was the thief.[53]

In Bengali, a *sadhu* is a holy man or ascetic; but as an adjective, the word means simply 'virtuous' or 'honest'. Whether consciously or not, Radice is repeating in English the substance of a Bengali pun—and conveying enough of the significance to a reader who does not know Bengali.

But clearly, this breaking of moulds can be salutary only where the host language outranks the source in the hierarchy of cultures. In the opposite instance, where a dominant source language invades the native practices of the host, the result will be to confirm the hegemony. There is or was a principle in historical philology known as Windisch's Law. In its basic formulation, it states simply that 'It is not the foreign language a nation learns that turns into a mixed language, but its own native language becomes mixed under the influence of a foreign language.' But in its classic application as borne out by historic evidence, this principle is held to operate primarily where the 'foreign' language belongs to a politically or culturally dominant nation and the 'native' language to a subordinate or subjugated one.[54] This phenomenon is evident in English *vis-à-vis* French after the Norman Conquest; several European languages *vis-à-vis* French after the eighteenth century; and the same languages *vis-à-vis* Anglo-American in the twentieth. It is equally evident in the Indian languages *vis-à-vis* English during and (perhaps even more) after colonial times. And as this is true of the languages themselves, so is it true of their literary and textual interaction, most directly through translation. What I am considering here is a conscious reversal of the process, whereby the subaltern language penetrates the dominant one.

This seems to point to a not infrequent prescription that a translation should read like a translation: that it should not coincide with the customary structures of either source or host language. This seems a fair enough proposition, with the impregnable logic of tautology—but it disconcerts me, for it seems most often to involve a formal devoir to political correctness rather than a genuinely creative interfusion. Such creativity is evident, if at all, not in translation as such but the wider translation of idiom, effectively the generation of a new idiom not organic to any current language, as in Naipaul or Rushdie's dialogue, and there it is fraught with an irony, even a patronization, that undermines its radical impact.

'When you are stronger,' someone who cannot be named is saying, 'a day at Elephanta, why not, a nice ride in a motor-launch, and all those caves with so-beautiful carvings; or Juhu Beach, for swimming and coconut-milk and camel-races; or Aarey Milk Colony, even!...' And Padma: 'Fresh air, yes, and the little one will like to be with his father.' And someone, patting my son on his head: 'There, of course, we will all go. Nice picnic; nice day out. Baba, it will do you good...'[55]

This extract from Rushdie merely subtilizes the technique used earlier by Naipaul in presenting the idiom of Indians in the Caribbean. In fact, in this example Naipaul's dialogue differs less from British Received Standard than Rushdie's does:

'Spitting on me, eh?' the god said. 'Go ahead. Why you don't spit now? Coming and laughing at our religion. Laughing at me when I do *puja. I* know the good I doing myself when I do *puja,* you hear.'[56]

These passages read like parodies of the kind of interfusion I am talking about. The very different idiom of the narrative framing in such dialogue, adopting or at least adapting British Received Standard, serves as a constant implicit critique. It is as though the parodic function seen in vernacular writing in colonial times, which I discussed earlier in this chapter, has been piquantly turned inside out. It is impossible to imagine the serious translation of Indian texts in Rushdie's literary idiolect. That would be on a par with saying that one must always talk baby-talk to a child or broken language to a foreigner.

A white man addressing a black, wrote Franz Fanon in 1952, 'behaves exactly like an adult with a child and starts smirking, whispering, patronizing, cozening.'[57] An episode from a recent Malaysian-English novel is relevant here. The heroine, an English-trained foreign-travelled Malaysian, has problems in talking to a Malay-educated girl in a travel bureau: they both ostensibly speak English, but the heroine feels it is not 'a common language' between them. She is amused when her mother speaks more effectively in 'a mixture of poor Cantonese and English patois'. Immediately afterwards, the heroine hears an American in the queue talking to his Chinese-Malay girlfriend in pidgin English, 'the sort picked up from comic books and late-night TV reruns of Fu-Manchu and Charlie Chan movies':

I felt incensed. I imagined he had a smirk on his face, as if it was a tremendous joke for him to be speaking so to this woman whom he had bedded and mated with ...[58]

Preposterous though the notion might seem, we need to reassure ourselves that this motive does not operate in the postcolonial texts I have cited. We need to assess seriously the growing practice of asserting the new international validity of 'Indian English' in terms of such texts. Yet alter the motive and circumstance, rather than the actual diction, syntax and morphology, and the same sublanguage can become the stuff of natural, authentic, sober discourse: a development less marked with Indian English, subcontinental or Caribbean, than with, say, Caribbean-French and Caribbean-English black writing. 'A sentence is but a chev'ril glove to a good wit. How quickly the wrong side may be turn'd outward!'[59]

The property of translation is to release with unique directness this to–and–fro debate about the nature and function of language. The Scepticism it generates lodges ultimately in the reception rather than the text, and can be directed by the latter only to a limited extent.

Clearly, I am stressing the consistently metalingual function of translation. Whatever a translated text might be 'about', it is always simultaneously about itself, about the working of language within it, on a plane that the original text was not. It purveys a process analogous to that of Aristotelian mimesis, whereby the substance of an experience is reproduced but also turned into something other than itself, something uniquely aware of its own form and thus transforming the nature of its being.

But let us consider Aristotle's angle:

... the reason of the delight in seeing the picture [considered as a work of imitation] is that one is at the same time learning—gathering the meaning of things, e.g. that the man there is so-and-so; for if one has not seen the thing before, one's pleasure will not be in the picture as an imitation of it, but will be due to the execution or colouring or some similar cause.[60]

Viewed in this light, it might be said that the relation between the source and host languages in translation differs in a crucial respect from the relation between a work of mimesis and its original. We are not forced to read the translation as a translation, with reference to the original—in fact, we usually lack access to the original and read a translation for that very reason. But the difference is not as fundamental as at first appears; indeed there is no real difference at all, for a translation necessarily refers outward to a cultural and intellectual entity other than itself; it suggests the original that we may not know at first hand.

The idea can be made clearer by reference to one of the most brilliant modern exponents of mimesis. In his book of that title, Erich Auerbach distinguishes between language 'of the foreground' and language 'fraught with background'.[61] The former mode is immersed in the present and surface implications of its language; the latter reaches beyond itself to suggestions, concealments, depths. One might adapt the distinction to apply to the language of an 'original' text *vis-à-vis* the language of translation. The former does not hark directly back to any other text; the latter of its nature points back to such a text if not a whole history of transmission. If the distinction does not hold entirely good, it is for the reason that makes me put 'original' within inverted commas and employ the adverb in 'hark *directly* back': as I shall argue in my next chapter, all texts look back at earlier texts, they are all in some sense translations or redactions of what has gone before. But in a formal translation, this feature obviously assumes a special dimension.

If a poem incorporates truth at two removes by Platonic formula, its translation stands three removes away. But this simple calculation is thrown awry by the translation bidding for an alternative version of the same reality at par with the source text, whatever truth-content that may imply. What the translation is simultaneously doing—in this obviously differing from the source-text—is to reflect also the latter, stand at *one* remove from the verbal entity of the source-text. Thus translations work to dispel the notion of truth-content in language. Instead, they foster the sense of a 'deep', layered, yet unrooted, expansive and changing continuum of alternative reality-structures, endlessly moderating one another, yet each recalcitrantly unique—in Heraclitean phrase, 'dying each other's life, living each other's death'.

When we read a translation, we are necessarily—however naively, however unbeknownst—reading something other than the translation. We are reading, in the fundamental sense of making an intellectual construct, the original text that we do not and very likely cannot read directly and literally. We are reading a reality that threatens to burst the confines of the language incorporating it. Finally, we are reading the act of reading and beyond that the act of writing, the construction and deconstruction of texts, the unpredictable courses taken by two interactive semiotic systems both operating, in different ways, outside their usual verbal and cultural orbits. We are exploring the undefined possibilities of verbalization, which are also undefined limitations. Translations tell us what we would otherwise not know; they make us question everything we might have thought we knew.

3

Translation and Creation

Rabindranath Thakur is one of the few major writers to have undertaken extensive translation of their own work. Beginning in 1912 with *Gitanjali (Song Offerings)*[62]—not a poem-for-poem equivalent of his Bengali work of the same name—he published a number of translations of his own poems and plays, anthologized later under the misleading title *Collected Poems and Plays of Rabindranath Tagore* (London: Macmillan, 1936). A few of these renderings have proved to be other people's work. The translations were made in increasing hurry, in pseudo-oriental, pseudo-poetic renderings now widely thought to have impaired rather than enhanced his reception in the West.

This negative though entirely tenable view of Rabindranath's self-made translations has, however, been gradually countered by a more positive one, now confirmed in detail by Sisir Kumar Das's elaborate critical edition of his *English Writings*.[63] It confirms the findings of earlier scholars that these English poems are far from being simple translations of the Bengali originals. Beyond local deviation—often considerable—Rabindranath has sometimes fused parts of separate Bengali poems into a single English one; added to or subtracted from the Bengali text; and in at least 26 cases, produced English texts for which no 'original' has been found, though a line or phrase here and there might recall some Bengali poem. There are also two volumes of lyrics and epigrams, aptly titled *Stray Birds* and *Fireflies,* with a particularly intricate play between parallel Bengali and English versions. The interaction is hard to unravel, but a number were undoubtedly first written in English. All this is besides the one work always known to have been first composed in English—*The Child,* a poem on Christ's nativity—which he later translated into Bengali; but again, the 'translation' is not exact.

The full picture radically alters our view of a poet from a marginalized culture ineptly hustling through a programme of translation as his ticket to the international literary circuit. His English poems—let us call them that—incorporate a large corpus of rewritings and recastings, rearrangements and cross-matchings, exegesis and fresh interventions, making up a concurrent, counterpoising creative process, a commentary on the dominant Bengali line, uniquely valuable as being from the poet's own pen. For the bilingual reader, the English texts afford continuous insights into the Bengali; they make him see the latter in new lights as Rabindranath himself did.

Going further, the English texts might provide a self-critique of Rabindranath's poetic being. His paintings are famously held to have fulfilled this role in a much more radical way. Without any formal training in art, Rabindranath began late in life to pour out a flood of cryptic, idiosyncratic, endlessly suggestive paintings, an expression of deep reserves of his creative self which the poet-guru could not bring himself to express consciously in his verbalizations. By contrast, his English writings might seem to provide the ultimate formalization of his public role of the poet as guru. Their surface intent is to disseminate and institutionalize the poet's work abroad. Thereby they work against their own profounder task of extending and deconstructing that very work, the Bengali corpus central to his reputation and his poetic being. The self-subverting creative boldness of the act is not apparent, but it is there. It operates beyond the usual contours of the colonial encounter-through-translation that I described in my first chapter.

As one delves deeper into Rabindranath's English poems, 'translation' seems more and more an inadequate and misleading term to designate them. They constitute nothing less than a parallel creative process. Yet unquestionably, they incorporate translation as the core activity through which all other functions are mediated—sometimes, apparently, to the near-exclusion of other functions.

Rabindranath's case is comparable to yet distinct from that of Vladimir Nabokov, who composed independently in Russian and English in two largely separate phases of his literary career, but conducted a programme of translations and even re-translations from each into the other. Some of the texts might have been considerably revised in translation. Nabokov valued the opportunity 'to abridge, expand, or otherwise alter or cause to be altered, for the sake of belated improvement, one's own writings in translation': he lamented that there was no word to denote the process.[64] But he does not question the priority of 'original' over 'translation': students of Nabokov have not identified any clear sense of the new language as such opening up new possibilities, or a protracted creative process that positively required bilingual execution. It is as though, under different circumstances, he might have carried out the revisions in the language he began with.

Even more clearly than Rabindranath, Nabokov may be said to differ in this respect from Samuel Beckett, whose creative activity is carried out *pari passu* in English and French with respect to the same work. Neither language is clearly foregrounded in his total corpus; neither is consistently the primary vehicle out of which he translates into the other. *Waiting for Godot* is not a 'translation' of the earlier *En attendant Godot,* nor, emphatically, *Endgame* of *Fin de partie;* but neither is *La dernière bande* of *Krapp's Last Tape* or *Oh! les beaux jours* of *Happy Days,* where the English versions came first.

Such being the case, priority of composition seems only an accident of circumstance in what is essentially a dual conceptualization. French and English provide concurrent media that enable Beckett to realize complementing, alternative forms of a seminal conception, set up an unusually self-extending, self-analytic context of composition through, as it were, an internal intertextuality. Through his twin vehicles, he can bring out two possibilities, exercise two choices where the average writer has but one.[65]

These various versions of auto-translation illustrate with unique clarity the process of extension, revision, critique and deconstruction invested in translation. Cases of self-translation also uniquely bring out the ambivalence of purpose inherent in the act of translation, which has sustained the core debate on translation down the ages. On the one hand lies the demand for 'faithfulness' or exactitude, with as little foregrounded intervention of the translator as possible. The latter's creative faculty is at work in a declaredly secondary way—intermediately, so to speak, between the 'original' writer and the 'passive' reader, scholar or exegetist. It is employed not to designedly modify the effect of the original but rather to preserve it to best purpose, to provide as equipollent a version as possible. This function of translation—which is obviously a definitive one—demands of the translator a basic humility, a submission of his creative being to another's. The auto-translator must cultivate a special detachment of being: the self that translates cannot be the self that had composed the original text. He might often approach his task as in some sense or other an ego-trip, an enhancement of his image as writer. Yet in his role as translator, he has to approach, from the outside and *post facto,* what he composed in another state of being. Of course I am talking about the verbal process of translation; but more fundamentally, also of the ontological primacy of the original text in any act of translation, whether by the original author or by another.

Yet with equal logic, the autotranslator can claim in unique degree the translator's function of modifying and remaking the original. This too, as we have seen, is an essential concomitant of the act of translation; it becomes explicit in the work of many practitioners declaredly undertaking creative translation—in other words, using the original text as the conduit for what they claim as their own independent and foregrounded creativity.

The autotranslator can claim a unique proprietory right to recast his 'own' work. Simultaneously, he can claim the proprietory right to explicate, i.e., to preserve and reaffirm that work, even if in practice he merely delimits its significance, consciously or unconsciously, by its redaction in another language. In other words, the autotranslator is illustrating the opposite impulses of the translator to preserve and to modify, to confine and to extend, to restrain and to exercise his own verbalizing faculty. He most obviously refutes any sharp opposition between Ezra Pound's two categories, 'interpretative translation' and 'the "other sort", ... where the "translater" [*sic*] is definitely making a new poem.'[66]

I have said earlier that the translator appears to be free of the 'anxiety of influence' but in fact shows a particular, perhaps fundamental version of that anxiety. By a sharper paradox, this is specially true of the autotranslator. The question of 'influence' appears not to apply to him at all; but he, more than any other translator, cannot escape his own creative presence. He cannot easily be other than himself; but the task of translation demands that he must be.

We seem impelled to conclude that the translator suffers in singular degree from the contrarious pulls of the anxiety of influence and what we might call the anxiety of deviance—the fear that he cannot write like his predecessor. To use another of Bloom's terms, the translator must specially guard against the charge of 'misreading'; yet he cannot proceed with his task unless he misreads, just like any other writer.

The range of creative misreading has been demonstrated in amazing detail in Douglas R. Hofstadter's *tour de force, Le Ton Beau de Marot: In Praise of the Music of Language* (London: Bloomsbury, 1997). With a luxuriant, self-indulgent sprawl, Hofstadter presents and expounds no fewer than 72 versions— translations, adaptations, imitations, parodies—of a single 28-line, 59-word poem by Clément Marot. Idiom and reference swing across the spectrum from medieval to pop, Gallic to Mid-West— yet each version is umbilically linked to Marot's original. The deviations are exuberantly created, as though to test how far they can range without severing that mother-bond.

In this contrariety of his stand, the translator once again magnifies the predicament of the creative writer working, as they all must, within a tradition: the need to conform and to advance, to write what is recognizable and fulfils a felt need, but what is at the same time unprecedented and satisfies an unsuspected want. He must be himself; he can never be truly himself, for his sensibility is a mass of readings and assimilations absorbed, modified, 'translated' in terms of each other and of the milieu of reception in which he has his being.

The degree of modification is always indeterminable, but at

times more obviously than at others. The clearest instances are those where the source culture is most distant from the target audience. Fitzgerald's Omar Khayyam, or Arthur Waley's translations from Chinese, are inevitably reduced in Western reception to the idiom of Western thought and utterance (which too will vary with the precise place and time). To what extent is such transmogrification effected by the translated text itself, and how much by factors in the reception of that text?

The literal departures are mensurable: a commentator familiar with the source can enlighten us. We know, for instance, that when the Victorian Khayyam sat under the bough with a girl, he made her 'sing' rather than merely 'sit', and omitted a thigh-bone of mutton from the amenities of the scene.[67] But what is lost and what substituted when Waley talks in an old Chinese poem of 'the town-houses of Royal Dukes', or makes Su Tung-P'o wish that his newborn son might become 'a Cabinet Minister'?[68] Or when Fitzgerald's Omar speaks of 'some buried Caesar' or, still more cross-culturally, of the 'predestination' with which he is 'round enmesh[ed]'?[69] Or for that matter when Rabindranath, translating his own play *Red Oleanders*, talks of the 'Jinn' of the dead wealth being mined from the ground, where the Bengali has a reference to the Tantric cult of corpses?[70]

However, the really telling cases are those embodying grades of determinacy, corresponding to variations of intention, where a bilingual or multilingual writer might be simultaneously (or at least potentially) a translator and an adapter or 'imitator', so that his work shows a graded scale of absorption. As one might expect, this multilingual and multicultural stand is most often not an individual but a general phenomenon of particular societies. One extensive body of examples can be found in the work of European humanists who wrote simultaneously in Latin (sometimes also

Greek) as well as a vernacular (rarely more than one), and moreover translated between any two or more of these languages. There are individuals who performed virtually this whole range of exercises: Filelfo and Poliziano, More and Reuchlin, Du Bellay and Milton. Certainly it was an accomplishment of the age as a whole.

We find here a spectrum of transfers and redactions. In the background, of course, is the ancient absorption of Greek models by the Romans (and that too is shorthand for a complex, graded process); and this leads to differences in approach, interpretation, rendering and imitation between classical Greek and classical Latin texts in the Renaissance. But beyond that we have in the Renaissance itself (a) translations from Greek into Latin; (b) translations from Greek and Latin into modern languages, and that either directly, or from Greek through Latin into vernacular, or from either classical language through one vernacular into another; (c) imitations of Greek and Latin texts. This last can be of many sorts: the formal 'imitation', the transference of a particular work into another setting or context; adaptation, the free reworking of an original with or without contextual transfer; or what purports to be an original poem in that it does not adhere consistently to one model or original, but echoes and interweaves various elements of classical provenance.

By this time, our minds might have begun to boggle. Yet anyone familiar with the ramifications of Renaissance literature will recognize this account as an authentic model of literary diffusion in the age. In a detailed study of as limited a form as the pastoral eclogue, I have found a range of absorption so intricate that the account above merely marks some major points along its course. With longer and more elaborate forms such as dramatic genres or the epic, the complexity is imaginable, or perhaps unimaginable.

And needless to say, the ramifications do not relate to the classical element alone; that is thrown into fluid combination with an indefinite number of other components and influences, operating to an indeterminate extent through actual translation.

Let us take one more Renaissance example: the Petrarchan love-convention, formally limited in its most familiar vehicle of lyric poetry but of immense structural and ideological significance. Petrarca's own *Rime* draw upon a range of models and precedents (not all of them directly known to Petrarca): some significant loci are earlier Tuscan poetry, the vast corpus of medieval romance, Provencal love-poetry, classical Latin love-poetry and its own Greek models, the covert presence of early Arabic poetry—as well as innumerable philosophical, mythographical and political elements. All these are purveyed, recycled and recharged through various languages. After Petrarca, again, his poems become the epicentre of a complex intertextual process involving new, lateral classical influences (most prominently the Ovidian love-elegy); new lyric models generated by Renaissance music; another mass of philosophic elements, Renaissance Platonism above all, and new gender politics. And of course, in the Renaissance as in the Middle Ages, there is the intricate commingling between such elite genres and systems and the popular lyric.

Petrarca is present everywhere and nowhere in this maze. We can regard 'translation' as a hopelessly inadequate term for this pervasive intertextual traffic across centuries; or we can ponder the implications of the term till it seems to absorb every nuance and extension of the process.

Let us take another example from another age and milieu. The works of Shakespeare exercised a striking influence on nineteenth-century Bengali culture, extending far beyond drama and formal literature; but confining oneself to the theatre for the moment, one finds again a wide trajectory of assimilation. There are formal translations, meant for stage rendering; retellings in prose narrative form; adaptations that might stick fairly closely to the original, but alter the names and settings to give the play an Indian garb; and extending from this, imitations and piecemeal borrowings of particular scenes, speeches or ideas, reaching finally to works that need have nothing specifically drawn from Shakespeare, but that would not have been written if Shakespeare's plays had not been known to the writer—and the audience and readers. More often than not, such knowledge drew on at least some contact with the original texts; but obviously, as the absorption increased (whether individually or communally), there would be more and more of a kind of osmosis through Bengali texts and performances. Again we find a model of multi-layered linguistic absorption. It might appear simpler than that in the European Renaissance, but it too is complicated by the presence of other models—the popular vernacular theatre or *jatra,* but also the classical Sanskrit drama. The Bengali elite was familiar with Sanskrit in that age, and the content of Sanskrit literature and Indian classical myth would have penetrated the general fabric of society much more deeply than today, appreciably though it still does. The elements of this traditional inheritance were drawn into the new Western-style, specifically Shakespeare-conditioned elite theatre, adding a new dimension to such assimilation.

My point in citing these complex instances, each spanning an entire age and culture, is to show how intricately translation intermeshes with the whole process of reading, absorption, interpretation and interpolation that constitutes formal verbal activity or 'literature'. Ultimately, it becomes a mirror and symbol of the process. We are all poets, said Carlyle, when we read a poem well.[71] More obviously, we are all translators when we do so

—translating often directly across languages, indubitably across the layered history of the poem's genesis, and at the same time across countries, cultures, periods and contexts, ultimately across individual sensibilities.

'The history of the great works of art,' writes Walter Benjamin,

tells us about their antecedents, their realization in the age of the artist, their potentially eternal afterlife in succeeding generations.[72]

To read a poem is really to 'read' the multichambered matrix of word and culture that engenders it. To write a poem is to make explicit, to extend actively into shaped and inscribed form, that same activity of translation. Eliot talks of

the importance of the relation of the poem to other poems by other authors, and ... the conception of poetry as a living whole of all the poetry that has ever been written.

But

The necessity that he shall conform, that he shall cohere, is not onesided; ... The existing order is complete before the new work arrives; for order to persist after the supervention of novelty, the *whole* existing order must be, if ever so slightly, altered; ... [T]he past should be altered by the present as much as the present is directed by the past.[73]

Verbal translation is a facet or outcrop of a continual mental and contextual translation. That is another way to define the intertextual constitution of any text. I read each text in, through and alongside every other text I have read; I read it not only in the language it is written in but in terms of all the others I know, and behind these all the languages I do not know but reach through translation, second-hand accounts, allusion and hidden presence. I view each language, as I do each text, in and through one or more others. My native tongue means differently to me for each new language I acquire. I comprehend and communicate by a finely graded sequence of mental cross-translations. And this entire terrain, ghostly Alps on Alps, moves in a fourth dimension as well: we translate, adjust and assess each work out of its original context into the terms of our own present.

The contents of my mind constitute an infinite range of translations—*versions*, 'turnings', a great mart of flexions, interfusions, mutually influenced deviations of identity. No two elements are in quite the same relation, just as no two stars in 'today's' night sky appear as they were at the same instant of time.

Similarly, no two translators (or the same translator in two works) stand in quite the same relation to the source text, or work the same equation between source language and target language, source culture and host culture. The spectrum I outlined above— from crib through 'transcreation' to free absorption—allows a range of functions, from high creativity to virtually secretarial transference, to enlist in the translators' army.

And ultimately, the individual equation underscores the social. This can be seen by considering contrastive examples of essentially the same phenomenon. Alexander Pope translated Homer; he imitated Horace. He retained the literal and formal appurtenances of Homeric Greece in the verbal idiom of his contemporary English, which implied modifying Homer's Hellenic ethos by the contemporary English one as well. But the change is concealed beneath a professedly 'straight' preservation of the Hellenic milieu: that is the direct subject of the work, and the Augustan-English ethos has to be extracted by a kind of pre-informed historical reading. This was true even for Pope's contemporaries, although the 'information' was in their case programmed, subconscious. They were imbibing their own ethos under cover of reading about the Greeks.

Obviously, the *Imitations of Horace* are differently oriented; but precisely how? It does not need saying that here there is no cover, or at most a transparent one. Pope is writing as he assumes Horace would have written had he lived in eighteenth-century England: that is roughly what the term 'imitation' implied in Pope's day. But equally, by preserving the Roman nomenclature and frame of allusion, Pope is retaining the Roman milieu as a controlling and assessing factor. Hence it is that although Horace's own poems were basically satirical, Pope can use their framework as a mock-heroic positive, a standard by which Pope's English milieu is found wanting and hence satirized on a different plane. The Latin supertext is applied ironically because it is being taken very seriously indeed. It provides the value-system governing the poem—in straight ethical terms, as well as the customary verbal and formal terms of neoclassical practice.

We find, then, a curious paradox. The translation that appears to preserve the ancient ethos literally and directly, undermines it by the terms of its verbal medium; while the imitation that seems to eschew such adherence actually preserves and values it. The controlling culture is in each case the opposite of the one we might expect. Homer becomes Pope; Pope aspires to become Horace, as Ben Jonson had done before him in *Poetaster*.

The lesson of this double-barrelled instance can be applied to a very different body of material: a curious phenomenon that I call 'anticipated translation'. I use the term for works that are not actually translations—but the fact that they are not is significant, for their material is such as one might have expected to encounter in another language, or translations therefrom.

The instance I have in mind is the recent inflorescence of Indian fiction in English. These novels and short stories present, in the

English language, a world in which that language is not normally used, and is not said to be used in the story. (Of course English is widely current in India, and such fiction often focuses on the English-speaking section of Indian society, but even then it assumes a wider range of reference: that is its whole intent and justification.) In other words, these books incorporate what we may call a 'cultural translation', and for that very reason do not require a verbal one to convey the society they write about. They assume the same encounter between nations as in actual translations from Indian languages into English. (I advisedly say 'between nations', as by its formal terms, such fiction is designedly addressed to an international Anglophone readership.)

The encounter is usually of the ambivalent kind I have described earlier, sharpened by the peculiarly active and penetrative role that English has played in India for nearly two hundred years. Such fiction shows—as all use of English in India does—on the one hand the organic absorption of an initially alien language, on the other a persistent modifying and alienating function of the language, turning the intrinsic terms of Indian culture into something other than themselves. However different stylistically, in political terms the process is not essentially different from that seen earlier this century in poets like Sarojini Naidu, who applied the idiom of exotic-orientalist Georgian English verse to Indian material:

> A kokila called from a henna-spray:
> *Lira! liree! Lira! liree!*
> Hasten maidens, hasten away
> To gather the leaves of the henna-tree.
> The *tilka's* red for the brow of a bride,
> And betel-nut's red for lips that are sweet;
> But, for lily-like fingers and feet,
> The red, the red of the henna-tree.[74]

The target readership of all such writing, past and present, includes English-reading Indians; but while reading, they too are approaching their milieu by a course that (while habitual for the portion to whom English has become the first or only language) is verbally circuitous and disorienting. This indirection might be turned to good purpose for critique, irony or indeed affirmation from an unaccustomed point of view. I have already discussed Naipaul or Rushdie's intricate critique of the Indian mental universe through a creative reworking of Indian English. In all such exercises, there is a strategy of deviance in more than one sense, a designed mismatch between the language of the text and the substance of what we may still call the source culture.

Certain writers of an earlier generation, like Raja Rao or R.K. Narayan, attempted a relatively 'straight', un-ironic presentation of Indian verbal and mental idioms in English. The tendency continues in contemporary writing—Sunetra Gupta's novels or, at a different level of utterance, in Ranga Rao's *Fowl-Filcher*. But such works are overshadowed by the sharper, more challenging metalingual critique of the writers we may call ironists.

Interestingly, this dimension might be emphasized in other writers by well-meant attempts to explain and annotate—the 'guide-book' element that creeps into such works as into 'annotational' translations, imparting an insidious remoteness even to material normal and commonplace in its context. With varying degrees of obliqueness, we find this feature prominent in such successful works as Vikram Seth's *A Suitable Boy* and Arundhati Roy's *The God of Small Things*. The tendency runs further in, say, Amit Chaudhuri's *A Strange and Sublime Address,* lightly fictionalized sketches of the placid surface of upper-middle-class Calcutta life, which would lose their *raison d'être* if translated into Bengali—or shall we say, if the material were retranslated into the language of the source culture.

It is hard to discuss this matter in language that is not value-loaded, and that does not appear to repeat the tedious and irrelevant argument that for an Indian to write in any language other than his ethnic mother-tongue is both impossible and unpatriotic if not immoral. At the same time, it must needs be said that to view these works in the right perspective, one has to consider their textual or verbal fabric in near-impossible separation from their representational or documentary function. The success of these works might have led to greater demand for translations of Indian-language texts, or a greater urge to translate such texts. The demand is growing, but so slowly as to raise fears of the opposite possibility: that the appearance of compelling English originals of Indian provenance might preclude the demand for translations from the Indian languages. That would be the *reductio ad absurdum* of Windisch's Law as applied to the hegemony of languages in a postcolonial situation: the assertive Indian-English achievements, apparently affirming a new world cultural order, might revalidate the old hegemony in new terms.

This is a matter of concern to that greater part of the Indian intelligentsia who lead bilingual or multilingual mental lives.[75] Interestingly, the concern has been forcibly echoed by at least one established Indian English writer, Amit Chaudhuri.[76] All the same, there is a serious danger that Indian writing in English should come to be viewed as 'Indian' literature *par excellence*. Factually or statistically, that is a patent absurdity; but the greater fear relates to the critical mindset implied.

This is likely to be much exacerbated by the currency of *The Vintage Book of Indian Writing 1947–97*, edited by Salman Rushdie and Elizabeth West.[77] Rushdie's preface reveals the limited critical perspective assumed in the book, owing to severe limitations in the compilers' knowledge of Indian languages. They have knowingly admitted only one non-English piece, from Saadat Hasan Manto's Urdu (coincidentially Rushdie's own Indian language). They are unaware that another piece, Satyajit Ray's 'Big Bill', has been translated from Bengali by the author himself. The selectors' choice was in any case confined to the (distressingly little) work available in English translation. They underestimate the (often truly poor) quality of these; and on this grossly inadequate base, argue for the overwhelming superiority of English to vernacular writing in India since Independence. This critical assessment is indistinguishable from a polemical apologia and manifesto for Indian writing in English—piquantly reversing Rushdie's own point in an earlier essay:

It is also worth saying that major work is being done in India in many languages other than English; yet outside India there is just about no interest in any of this work. The Indo-Anglians seize all the limelight.[78]

Indian writing in English assumes an author-reader interface very different from literature in the Indian languages. By virtue of its medium, it stands in a qualitatively different relation to Indian life and thought. Yet it is an authentic relation, socially valid in its own terms; of its formal or aesthetic validity there can be no question today. The Indian writer's world has been transformed since early imperial times when pioneers of modern Indian literature—the Bengali poet Michael Madhusudan Datta (Dutt) and novelist Bankimchandra Chattopadhyay, for instance—toyed with English in their youth but abandoned it for their native language. They drew upon a formal patriotism to prop up what was essentially a literary dismissal of their English work:

I travelled through a foreign land, mad for other men's property, turning
to beggary in an evil moment. I spent many days devoid of joy, body
and mind consigned to hunger and sleeplessness, sunk in fruitless
endeavour to honour that which deserves no honour.[79]

Beneath the general anti-English rhetoric, these lines by Michael
carry a gut judgment of the poet's own achievement in English, in
an age when the colonial imposition of the language enhanced its
use but prevented its total assimilation in Indian mental life. Clearly
this will not apply to Indian writers in English today.

A more germane comparison would be with Ngugi wa Thiong'o,
who gave up English for Gikuyu some twenty years ago. Indeed,
a comment by Ngugi on African English writers is equally
applicable to all English writers in ex-colonized states:

In the area of economics and geography, it is the raw materials of gold,
diamonds, coffee, tea, which are taken from Africa and processed in
Europe and then resold to Africa. In the area of culture, the raw material
of African orature and histories developed by African languages are
taken, repackaged through English or French or Portuguese and then
resold back to Africa.[80]

Ngugi's own stand marks a designed withdrawal from a
multiculturalism that is really monoculturalism, variation within a
hegemony. His stand has serious retrograde potential in that it
can cut off the artist from much of the conscious and explicit part
of his cross-affinities and interactions. It can imply not a reworking
of the hegemony but a mere opting-out.

Ngugi, of course, explicitly warns against such retrogression,
and stresses the imperative need for cultural borrowing and 'mutual
fertilization'.[81] His aim is to ensure the validation of each language
in its own terms which alone, at a later stage, can bring about a

genuine interfusion of languages and redefining of the cultural hegemony. Translation plays a vital part in Ngugi's scheme of languages, but he would not anticipate or preclude translation of his culture by writing in English at the present day. Rather, he would wrest the recognition that translations imply after a struggle through the entire process of composition and self-definition in the language of the soil.

By Ngugi's own account, such a projection is Utopian or at least remote in the African context. There is an obvious irony, of which he is well aware, that his plea for Kiswahili as *the* world language, composed in Gikuyu, should need to be translated into English and read at a BBC seminar. It is not as trenchant as the irony that this leading proponent of cultural Africanization should have to spend his days in exile in the West.

But these ironies and impediments would be less marked in the Indian, and most other Asian, contexts. There is nothing ascetic, nothing naive or primitivist about the *principle* of Ngugi's withdrawal from English. He is not, as it were, moving back from Babel to some enclosed localized Eden of verbal self-sufficiency. He is taking a deeply political stand that makes sense only in the context of the multilingual postcolonial cultural scene. He is so profoundly concerned with revising the hegemony, with striving for an equitable dispensation of cultures, that he is opting out of what he sees as a self-defeating process of 'anticipatory' cultural translation of the Kenyan reality into English.

Ultimately, the predicament of Ngugi is the same as that of the Indian-English novelist: not only in their provenance and bearings in a postcolonial world, but in the artistic location where they place and define themselves. They are both faced with an imperfectly multilingual, multicultural readership; they are both retreating into monolingual practice to meet the challenge of presenting their own culture in this uncongenial situation. But they are adopting opposite strategies *vis-à-vis* the multicultural 'translation' by whose operation creative writing and creative reading take place.

All texts and all readers are both monolingual and multilingual. A text, obviously written literally in one language in a given manifestation, faces a multilingual reader (as we all are to whatever extent, for reasons explained). Simultaneously, a multilingual text— multilingual by deeper provenance and affinity, by implicit 'translation' within it, and perhaps actual translation as well— encounters a dominantly monolingual reader. Substitute 'author' and/or 'culture' for 'text' and 'culture' for reader, work out all permutations between these terms, and the result will still hold good.

Translation—directly, literally meant—is mankind's simplest attempt to resolve this opposition in our cultural existence. But translation presupposes a substantial reality to be translated: it must be the encounter of two equipollent forces, the mutual reflection of light between two opaque objects that the trained eye alone can recognize and render, not the view through a transparent lens. Creation presupposes translation in some sense or other; but equally, creation, by definition, precludes translation. We are viewing my old paradox from the opposite perspective.

'Words, after speech, reach / Into the silence.'[82] There is a silence of suppression and inexpression and a silence of fulfilled, self-sufficient expression that feels no overt urge to communicate itself— just as there is a language in which we address the world and a language in which we address ourselves. We might still ponder the weary dictum that poetry is 'what is lost in translation'. This 'untranslatable' component arises from artistic intention and formal integrity, not the mere contingent semantic situations of source and target languages. It may be in this realm of silence, of desistence from translation, that we achieve our profoundest sense of alternative cultures and creative powers.

4

Translation and
Multilingualism

The ultimate translation myth is surely that devised by Borges about Pierre Menard, the Frenchman who recomposes portions of *Don Quixote*–in Spanish. So completely has he entered the being of the original that his rendering matches it word for word. The outcome is no different from a simple transcript of Cervantes's text; but Menard achieves this end by a total imaginative recreation of the text within himself, or we may say a recreation of himself in the light of the text until he feels and renders it from the depths of his own verbal being.

George Steiner takes the story to suggest the perfection of translation.[83] It may equally be read as exemplifying the futility of translation, its Sisyphean nature: the tautology constituted by a 'successful' translation, robbing it of its *raison d'être*. As Borges writes of his hero, 'He decided to anticipate the vanity awaiting all man's efforts; he set himself to an undertaking which was exceedingly complex and, from the very beginning, futile.'[84] But such a conclusion, logical enough, also logically prizes failure in such a futile task. The only value-added translation, it seems, is the imperfect one, for that alone takes us beyond the confines of the achieved, deviating from the source to contribute a text of its own. If Borges's Pierre Menard existed, he would clearly never find a publisher. His work would leave no record that was not ascribed to the original writer. The hypothetical 'exact' translation could serve only the practical purpose of conveying the text to someone unfamiliar with the source language; not the intellectual purpose of defining and illuminating its premisses. Fortunately, all translations are, as translations, more or less imperfect; the exact translation is impossible to achieve.

But our good fortune is on the conceptual plane; it is less apparent in actuality. Many root perturbations of human history have arisen from multiple translations, multiple deviations from some seminal text: each translation, each affirmation and onward transmission of the writ, was also an act of divergence, of subversion and dissent. Each new community of the spirit was a new-sprung nest of heresy.

Of the book that has controlled two thousand years of Western history, there have of course been innumerable translations. In the Christian world, it has had little impact in the original texts. Translations of the Bible fall into two categories: or more precisely, behind all translations of the Bible there have operated two motives in greatly varying proportions. They have all drawn on earlier versions—in the same language (from Tyndale to the Authorized Version to the Revised Version to the New English Bible) or in another (seminally the Vulgate), for the semantic and doctrinal field of the text is unchartable except through these. At the same time, they have all avowed the return to a source state, rectifying the distorting mediation of earlier versions, for only such rectification could justify a new translation.

A return to the source signification might imply a departure from the literal terms of the source text, as when Luther proposes 'to divest Moses of his Hebraisms'.[85] The authenticity sought might be rhetorical more than philological: 'to conceive rightly of the word and the feeling behind it and experience it in his heart', in Luther's phrase.[86] But this policy is not to avoid textual challenges, rather perhaps to meet them head-on. In a deceptively simple-sounding statement of method that essentially agrees with Luther's, the translators of the New English Bible write:

We have conceived our task to be that of understanding the original as precisely as we could (using all available aids), and then saying again in our own native idiom what we believed the author to be saying in his. We have found that in practice this frequently compelled us to make decisions where the older method of translation allowed a comfortable ambiguity. In such places we have been aware that we take a risk, but we have thought it our duty to take the risk rather than remain on the fence.[87]

In whatever way, each rendering of Holy Writ has thus been a reconfirmation and a revolution. The 'original' Biblical text is obviously ineluctable, for behind the Hebrew and Greek lie other languages (Aramaic); behind the canonical books, or even the canonical Apocrypha, lies an illimitable range of texts and traditions. More crucially for our purpose, even as regards the canonical text, the most iconoclastic rendering can assert its radicalism only by taking implicit cognizance of the whole line of translations, negotiating an unbroken course of ruptures, redefinitions that are equally overthrowals. It cannot disclaim this legacy, any more than a child can disclaim a parent.

The dissemination of the Bible thus generates a scenario sharply contrasting with that of, say, the Quran. Islamic practice vastly reduces the potential for such deviation by enjoining general use of the Arabic text, and indeed the Arabic language, throughout Islamic culture. With versions of the Bible, on the contrary, transfers of language constitute an inexhaustible source for modifications of doctrine or even narrative.

Hence the textually primitivist, back-to-the-source factor, among the two opposite compulsions I defined earlier, assumes a monolingualism and monosemy that paradoxically cut across languages and can be transmitted from one culture-context to another. It claims to translate yet not to translate, to retain in the target language the specific quality of the source so that the two are essentially one. Borges's hero translates out of Spanish into Spanish. Bible translations obviously are not unilingual (ipsolingual?) in this way: they are translations. But they claim as it were to be hermeneutically unilingual, mono-textual, non-interactive. They assume a single mental language, enshrining nothing less than the Word of God, operating across space and time: the clear line of an Edenic process of transmission rather than the net that the tongues of men have woven since Babel. 'O, 'tis not Spanish, but 'tis Heaven she speaks,' said Richard Crashaw of St. Teresa.[88] Heaven must speak the same way in all languages. The apostles needed the gift of tongues, but that could not impair the fixity of the Word they preached.

In the 2000-year course of Bible translation, and of ecclesiastical history and polity, such unilingualism of the mind, while implicitly fundamental, has been counterpointed by a practical awareness of the impure, plural and deviant transmission of scriptural text. All serious Bible translators have grappled with the problem of imperfect transmission, as well as the imperfection of all equivalence between languages. They have found in the gap between language and language, or between different versions in the same language, the genuine possibility of redefining (and arguably restoring, from a forgotten plane of authenticity) the terms of faith or the very components of scriptural discourse. In his famous letter to Martin

Dorp, Erasmus challenges Dorp's reservations about the Greek text of the New Testament, and the founding of a new Latin version on that basis:

I ask you, most learned Dorp, if what you write is true, why is it that Jerome, Augustine, and Ambrose had different readings from the ones that we have? ... What will you do in the face of such converging testimony, that is, when the Greek codices offer a different reading from ours, when Jerome in making citations uses that reading, when the most ancient Latin texts have the same reading, when its meaning fits better into the context? ... [I]t would be clear even to a blind man ... that the Greek was often poorly translated because of the ignorance or laziness of a translator, that often the authentic and true text has been corrupted by ignorant copyists ... or even changed by unskilled or inattentive ones. Who is more indulgent to error: the one who corrects and restores the mistakes, or the one who would sooner see a blunder added than removed?[89]

The latter group consists only of unworthy theologians, who 'fear that when they cite Sacred Scripture erroneously, as they often do, the authority of Greek or Hebrew truth will be thrown in their faces...'[90] Emendation of the text only confirms the permanence of the 'truth' it enshrines, even while it is a truth organically embodied in a particular language or utterance: 'Greek or Hebrew truth'.

In a shorter span, the persistence of an assumed unilingualism in and through actual translation can appear much more clearly. The outstanding modern instance would be the transmission of Karl Marx's texts, and (by no means the same thing) of Marxist texts and doctrines: the textualizing process whereby they have made up distinct versions of Marxist discourse for specific Marxist circles or polities. Hence, for such a widespread body of doctrine drawing on such a clear wellhead, we do not find the expected degree of interaction between a shared body of (often translated) texts; rather a series of parallel developments, each assuming an entrenched unilingualism even as it actually translates out of another language.

Lenin himself assuredly imbibed Marx primarily from the original German texts, although Russian translations existed for some of them and he may, of course, have known these. Like all educated Russians of his generation, he was familiar with German and French, and to a lesser degree, English.[91] Mao dze-Dong, on the contrary, absorbed Marx (and Lenin) from the small number of texts available in Chinese translation. He seems indeed to have relied in good measure on secondary studies and exegeses rather than the works themselves.[92] It is fascinating to ponder on the 'translation factor' in the evolution of Mao's radically distinct version of Marxism-Leninism, what in one celebrated phase of development termed itself the 'Sinification of Marxism'. Certainly, language is cited as a crucial factor in defining the process: in the words of Liu Shao-ch'i,

Mao Tse-Tung's great accomplishment has been to change Marxism from a European to an Asiatic form. Marx and Lenin were Europeans; they wrote in European languages about European histories and problems, seldom discussing Asia or China. ... Mao Tse-Tung is Chinese; he analyzes Chinese problems and guides the Chinese people in their struggle to victory.[93]

And Mao himself talks in terms of a specific Chinese idiom:

We must put an end to writing eight-legged essays on foreign models; there must be less repeating of empty and abstract refrains; we must discard our dogmatism and replace it by a new and vital Chinese style and manner, pleasing to the eye and to the ear of the Chinese common people.[94]

How much, we may ask, is Mao's crucial redefinition of the revolutionary role of the peasantry *vis-à-vis* the industrial proletariat owing to the rendering of *bourgeois* and *proletariat* in Chinese as the 'propertied' and 'propertyless' classes, with no direct bearing upon Marx's own European model of an industrial economy? Stuart Schram has suggested the possibility.[95]

In other Asian countries with communist regimes or prominent communist movements—including such Indian states as Kerala and West Bengal—Marx's texts, and other Marxist texts, have circulated largely in local-language translations purveyed by the subsidized foreign-language publishing network of erstwhile Soviet Russia. In every case, the reception of Marx has been largely unilinear, realized through a local language whose relation with Marx's original is more or less removed, more or less tangential. More significantly, their relations with *each other* have also been variable: sometimes considerable—like the controlling influence of Mao-dze-Dong on radical Indian Marxism in the 1960s—but often minimal, through intermittent political contact rather than textual comparison. Occasionally, in countries with strong bilingual or multilingual bases such as India, some interaction might have taken place, especially among the urban intelligentsia, who have access to English versions or even original texts in German or Russian.

With these reservations, one can say that the various lines of Asian communism run disjunct textual courses, each through its own linguistic channel. The notional textuality of a prototype-ideology is fragmented into distinct textual traditions, differing from each other and often in relations of reaction or conflict. Collectively, they differ from the pattern of European communism, which obviously operates in a radically different relation to the seminal Marxist texts, not to mention the distinctive politics of the

region. Indeed, West European communist theory can regard even
the Russian model as deviating from the textually authentic Marxist
construct. Thus a number of competing Marxisms have been
generated, each within its own linguistic capsule and concomitant
ethos, which invariably predate the arrival of Marx.

There is a fundamental difference between cultures of text, such
as traditional Christian civilization and Marxist polities, and cultures
of praxis such as modern capitalism. The latter has no defined,
textualized ideology; its ethos is extensible in a protean, amorphous,
arguably vacuous manner. The former textualizes its ethos and
professes to conduct itself by the terms of that text. (In China, the
relative lack of access to Marx's text called forth other canonical
texts in the form of Mao dze-Dong's own writings, epitomized in
the Red Book.) Such cultures are more or less single-noted, more
or less prescriptive, and this restriction links up with a verbalization
that is implicitly unilingual.

As I have argued earlier, all textualization, all reception of the
word can be seen as fundamentally 'translation'; but markedly
text-reliant cultures would suppress this 'translation factor' when
conceptualizing their ethos. They would see their world as verbally,
therefore ethically monochromatic, while cultures of praxis
incessantly shift in hue, like the colours of a psychedelic dream.
Gayatri Chakravorty Spivak has defined 'the received dogma of
the freedom of the aesthetic and literature's refusal to soil itself by
rendering service to the state—when that very refusal is the greatest
service that it can render to a polity that must disguise the extraction
of surplus value as cultural dynamism.'[96] Both these ethoses would
deny the philosophic, catholic, yet dedicated and even
interventionist scepticism of the multilingual vision that I have
proposed as the aptest mindset for the translator.

I am distinguishing between monolingualism, the literal state of knowing or using only one language, and what I call unilingualism, a mindset or ethos that operates only in terms of one language. Unilingualism is entirely compatible with knowledge, even deep knowledge, of several languages; indeed, it is often seen at its most entrenched and intolerant in multilingual situations.

The true curse of Babel is not that humans cannot comprehend one another's language. It is that they can, but then oppose or resent what the others say—that they comprehend but do not understand the Other. Literal translation, the task of what in English is ineptly called the interpreter, does not obviate the risk. Wars between nations have been mediated through heralds and messengers. Where one human race has utterly failed to comprehend the tongue of another, they have gunned the latter down as animals; where they have comprehended and differed, they have called down the profounder, more recondite destruction reserved by humans for one another.

A multilingual society obviously finds the mechanical task of translation easier—not only for languages within its ambit but, owing to the verbal faculties fostered, others as well. *Mutatis mutandis,* this is true of linguistic interaction across societies and nations and indeed of the entire international traffic of translation. Yet the interaction of nations and cultures, verbally as in other modes, has been consistently imperfect, hegemonic and even hostile. The potential intricacy of such hegemonies may be best illustrated from the Indian linguistic scene, for it incorporates a multi-level, wheel-within-wheel hierarchy of Indian languages set in a wider context of English and other European languages, with yet others such as Arabic and Persian. The interpenetration of these elements is too complex to be traced. Actual translation plays only a subsidiary role.

The situation in Europe provides interesting parallels as well as crucial differences, and the political drawing-together of the continent is bound to revolutionize the interaction of its languages.[97] The reverse process shows in the sector of South Asia most affected by the post-imperial partition of the subcontinent. Western or Indian Bengal shares a common language with Bangladesh, but clear lines of divergence are showing after fifty years of political and ideological separation. If the factors behind such divergence persist, the languages of the two parts might one day come to differ from each other as decisively as Bengali does today from the geographically and historically proximate languages of Assamese and Oriya.

Both South Asia and Europe provide elaborate models for linguistic interaction and interpenetration, far beyond the simple verbal traffic of geographically proximate language-groups. As the annals of both regions illustrate, this has never precluded animosity and bloody hostility at any point of history, or the creation of political and economic hegemonies. Rather, multilingualism has been adapted to the demands of such a hegemony; it has served as its basis and its rationale.

Hence the relevance of an alternative view of the verbalization of culture, leading us onto a plane of interactive mental process beyond texts and the textualization of cultures. The act of translation assumes that individual readers might know only one language; equally, it assumes the need and the possibility of moving from one language-world to another. It establishes the interdependent existence of world on world, the presence of one verbal world in and behind another, with yet others in attendance. This is the ideology of translation I have tried to build up here.

When Rabelais's Pantagruel first meets the scintillating rogue Panurge, the latter is dying of hunger. He asks for bread in no fewer than thirteen languages (including three non-existent ones) to no effect; in the end, he divulges almost casually under question that he is a Frenchman like his interlocutors.[98] Lewis Carroll evokes such a case more succinctly in *The Hunting of the Snark:*

> I said it in Hebrew—I said it in Dutch—
>   I said it in German and Greek:
> But I wholly forgot (and it vexes me much)
>   That English is what you speak![99]

Multilingualism does not ensure success in communication. Where there is an infinity of monolingual lines of speech, one needs to hit the right one rather than cross tracks. This is the problem of multilingualism in a monolingual/unilingual universe.

By way of contrast, let me cite another, real-life and by no means untypical model of multilingualism. George Steiner says of himself:

[O]ne of the 'languages' inside me, probably the richest, is an eclectic cross-weave whose patterns are unique to myself though the fabric is quite palpably drawn from the public means and rule-governed realities of English, French, German, and Italian.[100]

Very many Indians can match this command of language, if rarely at Steiner's level of perception. So can many nations of South-East Asia, no doubt among others.

As Steiner's account bears out, a person who knows four languages is not some kind of outer skin enclosing four homunculi speaking one language each. The various language-skills mingle to form a unique verbal being at a specific location in space and time. What is true of the individual is true of the collective entity. Linguistic interaction is not a seamless continuity but an endless sequence of encounters, each unique, each exposing a new interface—endless singularities rather than one singleness. We can gather them into models of translinguistic or supralinguistic transactions, broad categories of verbal perception, without committing ourselves to monolithic universals which the ideology of translation necessarily denies.

I have argued against a commonalty of perception in the epistemological sense. I have advanced translation as a major premiss in denying any such universal. This does not negate the fact that many memorable human values, including this very anti-essentialism, have been generated by the encounter of languages and transference between them. I do not mean the instrumental function of the encounter, its mere conveyance of certain pre-set significations from one environment to another, but the generative function of the encounter itself, issues raised by and in the process of translation.

This opening out of philosophic doors from the corridors between languages was a task first purposefully undertaken by the Renaissance humanists. Since then, by a glib yet logical and historically-valid quibble across centuries, it has advanced itself as a significant function of humane and humanist cultures. Of course there is a quibble in the jump from verbal and textual exercise to ethical value, hence the establishment of the former as a key human activity; but it is a quibble borne out by the terms of the pursuit. I am pleading to uphold this association, to imbue the verbal exercise with ethical value on a plane quite different from the one I earlier held suspect, where the verbal process was itself endowed with value-functions like 'loyalty' and 'truth'.

Robert J. Matthews makes a pertinent point in a perceptive essay. He questions the efficacy, if not the validity, of any epistemologically-based rationale of translation, any assumption that it renders from one language to another the notion of an objective, empirically valid reality. Instead, he proposes to test linguistic equivalence by equivalence of psychological response in the recipients:

I suspect that translation is determinate only relative to a given psychological theory, so that while for any translator ... there is a uniquely correct translation scheme for any given set of utterances, there is no absolutely correct scheme.[101]

Unlike many other anti-humanist, 'radical' theories of language and culture, recent translation theory has moved away towards pragmatic models geared to formal linguistic analysis in the interest of practical communication. It commonly discounts the distinction between scientific/factual and poetic texts. It is thus at risk of undermining the philosophic, hence ethical dimension of translation, the awareness of language and meaning beyond the semantic confines of the text under translation.

I would submit that a recognition of these factors would enhance the practical, communicative function of translation. For in the act of translation, the significant divergence I have continually spoken of operates in a way quite contrary to the apparent purport of my account. The translator might hope for successfully creative divergence—he cannot avoid divergence after all. But insofar as he professes any function of rendition—and this too he cannot abjure if he is to call himself a translator—he must control this divergence, manipulate its transformative and disjunctive function to follow the semiotic trajectory of the source text, rather as some modern railways ride along a magnetic track they do not touch. As Walter Benjamin puts it,

It is plausible that no translation, however good it may be, can have any significance as regards the original. Yet, by virtue of its translatability the original is closely connected with the translation.[102]

The divergence is undeniable; it is necessarily incorporated in the rendition; but it is not centrifugal. Rather, it points back to the original from which it deviates, but shows up the latter in a new light in terms of the deviation, displays it against a new linguistic order.

To return to the paradox with which I set out, translation draws us away from the source, but equally draws us towards it; without the translation, we would have been oblivious of the source. It turns something else into ourselves; it turns ourselves into something other than ourselves. The translator is an egotist who posits himself as the channel of transmission for a prexistent work or writer; he exemplifies a unique humility and self-mortification by submitting his verbal being to parameters that need not, cannot coincide with those of the source text but are at least regulated by the latter.

Notes

Chapter I

1. See the references in Susan Bassnett, *Comparative Literature: A Critical Introduction,* Oxford: Basil Blackwell, 1993, pp.140–41. See also Barbara Johnson, 'Taking Fidelity Philosophically' in Joseph F. Graham (ed.), *Difference in Translation,* Ithaca: Cornell University Press, 1985, pp.142–4.

2. Jagannath Chakravorty, 'Translate Me', trans. Supriya Chaudhuri in Visvanath Chatterjee (ed.), *Word for Word: Essays on Translation in Memory of Jagannath Chakravorty,* Calcutta: Papyrus, 1994, p.126.

3. John Donne, 'The Triple Foole', as in *The Elegies and Songs and Sonnets of John Donne,* ed. Helen Gardner, Oxford: Clarendon Press, 1965 rpt. 1978, p.52.

4. Jacques Derrida, 'Plato's Pharmacy' (French original 1968), in *Dissemination,* trans. Barbara Johnson, London: Athlone Press, 1981 rpt. 1993, p.72.

5. Jacques Derrida, 'Structure, Sign and Play in the Discourse of the Human Sciences' (French original 1966), in *Writing and Difference,* trans. Alan Bass, London: Routledge & Kegan Paul, 1978 rpt. 1985, p.289.

6. Pope's *Iliad* 15:540–63. As in *The Poems of Alexander Pope,* Twickenham edn., vol. 8, ed. Maynard Mack, London: Methuen, 1967.

7. *Iliad* Book 15, trans. E.V. Rieu, Harmondsworth: Penguin, 1950, p.284.

8. *The Greek Bucolic Poets,* ed. and trans. J.M. Edmonds, London & Cambridge, Mass.: Heinemann & Harvard University Press, 1912 rpt. 1960, p.445.

9. *Greek Pastoral Poetry,* trans. Anthony Holden, Harmondsworth: Penguin, 1974, p.187.

10. José Ortega y Gasset, 'The Misery and the Splendor of Translation', trans. Elizabeth Gamble Miller in Rainer Schultz & John Biguenet (ed.), *Theories of Translation: An Anthology of Essays from Dryden to Derrida,* Chicago: University of Chicago Press, 1992, p.109.

11. See David Lodge, *Small World,* London: Martin Secker & Warburg, 1984: Part I ch.1, Part III ch.1.

12. Jacques Derrida, 'Des Tours de Babel', trans. Joseph F. Graham in *Difference in Translation,* ed.cit. note 1, p.171.

13. R.T. Davies (ed.), *Medieval English Lyrics: A Critical Anthology,* London: Faber & Faber, 1963 rpt. 1971, p.160. Spellings have been standardized, except for the archaic 'brenneth' (burneth).

14. Manabendra Bandyopadhyay, Sukanta Chaudhuri & Swapan Majumdar (ed.), *Voices from Bengal: Modern Bengali Poetry in English Translation,* New Delhi: Sahitya Akademi, 1997.

15. See Gayatri Chakravorty Spivak, *In Other Worlds: Essays in Cultural Politics,* New York: Methuen, 1987, p.187.

16. The Italian version of *The Fugitive* was revised by Giacinta Bon Martini and Giuseppe Tucci from the original drafts by Pramathanath Roy, who presumably worked from the Bengali. Manuscript Italian translations have been made directly from the Bengali by Flavio Poli and Mario Prayer. (I owe this information to Indrani Das of the Department of English and Other Modern European Languages, Visva-Bharati.)

17. Cees Nooteboom, 'When Translators Are as Important as Authors': *Washington Post Book World,* rept. *The Asian Age,* Calcutta, 26 August 1997.

18. Bernard S. Cohn, *Colonialism and Its Forms of Knowledge: The British in India,* Delhi: Oxford University Press, 1997, pp.21–2. Cf. p.53.

19. Homi K. Bhabha, 'The Voice of the Dom', *TLS* no.4923, 8 August 1997, p.14.

20. Aniket Jaaware, 'Translation and Its Theories: Some Ideas and Questions', *Jadavpur University Essays and Studies* vol.11, Calcutta, 1997, p.28.

21. Edward Fitzgerald, letter to E.B. Cowell, 1857. Cited in André Lefevere, *Translation/History/Culture: A Sourcebook,* London: Routledge, 1992, p.80.

22. See Ernst Robert Curtius, *European Literature and the Latin Middle Ages,*

trans. Willard R. Trask, London: Routledge & Kegan Paul, 1953 rpt. 1979, p.29.

23. See Edward W. Said, *Orientalism: Western Conceptions of the Orient,* London: Routledge & Kegan Paul, 1978, Part 1 ('The Scope of Orientalism'), sections 3 & 4. Cf. Cohn above (note 18) on the reification of the colonized Indian culture.

24. Bassnett, op.cit. note 1, pp.10, 143, citing Lawrence Venuti (ed.), *Rethinking Translation,* London: Routledge, 1992.

Chapter II

25. *The Select Nonsense of Sukumar Ray,* trans. Sukanta Chaudhuri, Calcutta: Oxford University Press, 1987.

26. Ferdinand de Saussure, *Course in General Linguistics,* trans. Wade Baskin, ed. C. Bally, A. Sechehaye & A. Reidlinger, 1959, rpt. London: Fontana/ Collins, 1974, pp.66–7. See also Ortega y Gasset, op.cit. note 10: the linguist's discourse, pp.106–8.

27. Ortega y Gasset, ibid. p.97.

28. Translated by the present author from 'Ingrajstotra' in *Lokrahasya,* 1878, as in Bankimchandra Chattopadhyay, *Bankim Rachanabali* vol. 2, Calcutta: Sahitya Samsad, 1956 rpt. 1964, pp. 9–10.

29. Rajshekhar Basu, 'Ulat-Puran', *Kajjali,* Calcutta: M.C. Sarkar & Sons, 1928.

30. Rajshekhar Basu, 'Swayambara', ibid.

31. William Shakespeare, *The Tempest* I.ii.355–8: as in *Complete Works* ed. Peter Alexander, London: Collins, 1951 rpt. 1978.

32. N.K. Sandars, 'Translating the Translators: Peculiar Problems in Translating Very Early Texts', in William Radice & Barbara Reynolds (ed.), *The Translator's Art: Essays in Honour of Betty Radice,* Harmondsworth: Penguin, 1987, p.143.

33. Rabindranath Thakur, 'The Patriot', as in *The English Writings of Rabindranath Tagore,* ed. Sisir Kumar Das, vol.2, New Delhi: Sahitya Akademi, 1996, p.268. The English title does not translate the Bengali 'Samskara' ('change' or 'reform', but also 'convention' or 'orthodox belief').

34. See, e.g., Arthur Cooper's Introduction to his translation of *Li Po and Tu Fu,* Harmondsworth: Penguin, 1973 rpt. 1976, pp. 53–5, 79–82.

35. Gilbert Murray, Preface to Aristotle, *On the Art of Poetry,* trans. Ingram

Bywater, Oxford: Clarendon Press, 1920 rpt. 1932, p.4.

36. Vladimir Nabokov, 'Problems of Translation: *Onegin* in English' (first published 1955), in *Difference in Translation,* ed.cit. note 1, p.143.

37. Michel de Montaigne, *Essays* II:12 ('Apology for Raymond Sebond'), as in *The Complete Essays of Montaigne,* trans. Donald M. Frame, Stanford: Stanford University Press, 1958 rpt. 1965, p.392.

38. Montaigne, *Essays* I:23 ('Of Custom, and not easily changing an accepted law'): ibid. p.86.

39. Montaigne, *Essays* I:37 ('Of Cato the Younger'): ibid. p.169.

40. Montaigne, *Essays* I:31 ('Of Cannibals'): ibid. p.152.

41. William Shakespeare, *King Lear* III.iv.104: ed.cit. note 31.

42. *Petrarch's Lyric Poems,* trans. & ed. Robert M. Durling, Cambridge, Mass.: Harvard University Press, 1976, Preface, p.ix.

43. Charles Mills Gayley, 'What Is Comparative Literature?', *Atlantic Monthly* 92, 1903, as quoted in Bassnett, *Comparative Literature.*

44. Walter Benjamin, 'The Task of the Translator', in *Illuminations* (German original, 1955), ed. Hannah Arendt, trans. Harry Zohn, 1970; rpt. London: Fontana/Collins, 1977, p.74.

45. Umberto Eco, *The Search for the Perfect Language* (Italian original 1993), trans. James Fentress, Oxford: Blackwell, 1995, pp.344–9.

46. George Steiner, *After Babel: Aspects of Language and Translation,* London: Oxford University Press, 1975.

47. George Steiner (ed.), *Poem into Poem,* Harmondsworth: Penguin, 1970, p.29.

48. Andrew Benjamin, *Translation and the Nature of Philosophy: A New Theory of Words,* London: Routledge, 1989.

49. Alberto Manguel, *A History of Reading,* London: Flamingo, 1997, p.276.

50. Rudolf Pannitz, *Die Krise der europäischen Kultur,* as quoted in translation by Rainer Schultz & John Biguenet in the Introduction to *Theories of Translation,* ed.cit. note 10, p.8. Cf. Friedrich Schleiermacher's remarks ('On the Different Methods of Translating', German original 1813: ibid. p.42) on translations that bring the reader to the writer, and those that bring the writer to the reader; and Ortega y Gasset, 'The Misery and the Splendour of Translation': 'It is only when we force the reader from his linguistic habits and oblige him to move within those of the author that there is actually translation.' (ibid. p.108)

51. Rabindranath Tagore, *Selected Poems,* trans. William Radice, Harmondsworth: Penguin, 1985, p.94.

52. 'The Lady of the Sea', trans. Humayun Kabir, in *One Hundred and One Poems by Rabindranath Tagore,* Bombay: Asia Publishing House, 1966, p.118.

53. Tagore, *Selected Poems,* ed.cit. note 51, p.57.

54. See Otto Jespersen, *Language: Its Nature, Development and Origin,* London: George Allen & Unwin, 1922 rpt. 1950, p.208.

55. Salman Rushdie, *Midnight's Children,* London: Jonathan Cape, 1981, p.206.

56. V.S. Naipaul, *A House for Mr. Biswas,* 1961, rpt. Harmondsworth: Penguin, 1976, p.136.

57. Franz Fanon, *Black Skin, White Masks* (French original, 1952), trans. Charles Lam Markmann, 1967, rpt. New York: Grove Press, 1968.

58. Chuah Guat Eng, *Echoes of Silence,* Kuala Lumpur: Holograms, 1994, p.224. Cf. this anecdote from the memoirs of an ICS officer of British India, about an Indian who wrote excellent English but chose to speak it haltingly before Englishmen. He explained his policy thus:

I have told you often about Mr and Mrs Roxburgh when he was SDO here. ... I noticed that whenever I spoke good English ... Mrs Roxburgh looked a little vague. But whenever I reverted to halting and pidgin English she warmed up. One day she actually exclaimed, 'Deben Babu, I like your perfect broken English so much, it sounds so good!' I'll tell you what, Englishmen ... really want to hear perfect broken English from you. From that day I gave up my college accent and my acceptability was never in doubt. (Asok Mitra, *Towards Independence, 1940–1947: Memoirs of an Indian Civil Servant,* Mumbai: Popular Prakashan, 1991, p.71.)

59. William Shakespeare, *Twelfth Night* III.i.11–12: ed.cit. note 31.

60. *Poetics* ch.4: ed. cit. note 35, p.29.

61. Erich Auerbach, *Mimesis: The Representation of Reality in Western Literature,* trans. Willard R. Trask, Princeton: Princeton University Press, 1953 rpt. 1973, pp.7, 11–12.

Chapter III

62. Rabindranath Tagore, *Gitanjali (Song Offerings),* London: India Society, 1912; Macmillan, 1913.

63. *The English Writings of Rabindranath Tagore,* ed.cit. note 33.

64. Vladimir Nabokov, Foreword to *Invitation to a Beheading:* see Jane Grayson, *Nabokov Translated: A Comparison of Nabokov's Russian and English Prose,* Oxford: Oxford University Press, 1977, p.9.

65. Cf. Brian T. Fitch, 'The Relationship between *Compagnie* and *Company:* One Work, Two Texts, Two Fictive Universes', in A.W. Friedman, C. Rossman and D. Sherzer (eds.), *Beckett Translating / Translating Beckett* (University Park: Pennsylvania State University Press, 1987), p.32:

Since *Company* and *Compagnie* manifestly cannot be substituted for one another, the sum total of the two texts is necessarily greater than either of them. What is more, the result of bringing the two together to study the reciprocal relationship brought about by their coexistence produces something *other* than such a sum total ... for in the process of adding them together, irreconciliable differences remain.

66. Ezra Pound, 'Cavalcanti', *Literary Essays,* London: Faber & Faber, 1954, p.200.

67. Edward Fitzgerald, 'Rubaiyat of Omar Khayyam of Naishapur', stanza 11: as in Francis Turner Palgrave (ed.), *The Golden Treasury of ... Songs and Lyrical Poems ... with Additional Poems,* London : Oxford University Press, 1914 rpt. 1931, p.344. This is the text of Fitzgerald's first edition. For the departures from the Persian, see Edward Heron-Allen, *Edward Fitzgerald's Rubaiyat of Omar Khayyam with Their Original Persian Sources,* London: Bernard Quaritch, 1899, pp.22–5.

68. *One Hundred and One Chinese Poems,* trans. Arthur Waley, London: Jonathan Cape, 2nd edn., 1962, rpt. 1974, p.24 ('Seventeen Old Poems', no.3), p.77 (Su Tung-p'o, 'On the Birth of His Son').

69. Fitzgerald, op.cit. note 67, stanzas 18, 57. See Heron-Allen, op.cit. note 67, pp.32-5, 118–19.

70. Rabindranath, *English Writings,* ed.cit. note 33, vol.2 p.212.

71. Thomas Carlyle, *On Heroes and Hero-Worship,* 1841; rpt. London: Oxford University Press, 1904 rpt. 1963, p.107 ('The Hero as Poet').

72. Benjamin, op.cit. note 44, p.71.

73. T.S. Eliot, 'Tradition and the Individual Talent', *Selected Essays 1917–1932,* London: Faber & Faber, 1932, pp.17, 15.

74. Sarojini Naidu, 'In Praise of Henna', *The Sceptred Flute: Songs of India,* Allahabad: Kitabistan, 1943, p.13. This is one of a group of similar poems

curiously placed under the heading 'Folk Songs'.

75. See, for instance, Harish Trivedi, 'India and Post-Colonial Discourse', in Harish Trivedi & Meenakshi Mukherji (ed.), *Interrogating Post-Colonialism: Theory, Text and Context,* Shimla: Indian Institute of Advanced Study, 1996.

76. Amit Chaudhuri, 'Beyond the Language of the Raj', *TLS* no.4923, 8 August 1997, p.17.

77. Salman Rushdie & Elizabeth West (ed.), *The Vintage Book of Indian Writing 1947–1997,* London: Vintage, 1997.

78. Salman Rushdie, ' "Commonwealth Literature" Does Not Exist', *Imaginary Homelands: Essays and Criticism,* London: Granta, 1991.

79. Michael Madhusudan Datta, Sonnet: 'Bangabhasha', lines 3–7, in *Chaturdashpadi Kabitabali.* Translated by the present author.

80. Ngugi wa Thiong'o, 'Creating Space for a Hundred Flowers to Bloom' (1990 lecture at Yale University), in *Moving the Centre: The Struggle for Cultural Freedoms,* London: James Currey, 1993, p.20.

81. Ibid. p.22.

82. T.S. Eliot, 'Burnt Norton' V, *Four Quartets: Cullected Poems 1909–1962,* London: Faber & Faber, 1963 rpt. 1968, p.194.

Chapter IV

83. Steiner, *After Babel,* ed. cit. note 46, pp.70–72.

84. Jorge Luis Borges, 'Pierre Menard, Author of the *Quixote*', *Labyrinths,* trans. Donald A. Yates & James E. Irby, 1966, rpt. Harmondsworth: Penguin, 1974, pp.70.

85. Quoted in H.O. Burger, 'Luther as an Event in Social History', *Martin Luther: 450th Anniversary of the Reformation,* Bad Godesberg: Inter Nationes, 1967, p.127.

86. Ibid. pp.125–6.

87. *The New English Bible: New Testament,* Oxford: Oxford University Press & Cambridge University Press, 1961, Introduction, pp.viii–ix.

88. Richard Crashaw, 'An Apology for the Foregoing Hymn' (i.e., 'A Hymn to the Name and Honour of the Admirable Saint Teresa'), line 23: Crashaw, *Poems,* ed. J.R. Tutin, London: George Routledge & Sons, no date, p.136.

89. Desiderius Erasmus, Letter to Martin Dorp, May 1515, as in *Christian Humanism and the Reformation,* trans. & ed. John C. Olin, New York: Harper

& Row, 1965, p.84.

90. Ibid. p.88.

91. See Nadezhda K. Krupskaya, *Memories of Lenin,* trans. E. Verney, 1930, rpt. Allahabad: India Publishers, no date, pp.146, 147–52.

92. See the account in Stuart Schram, *Mao Tse-Tung,* Harmondsworth: Penguin, 1966 rpt. 1969, ch.3.

93. Statement by Liu Shao-ch'i to Anna Louis Strong, 1946; quoted in Stuart Schram, *The Political Thought of Mao Tse-Tung,* New York: Frederick A. Praeger, 1963 rpt. 1965, p.56.

94. Translated from *On the New Stage,* 1939, ch.7: see ibid., p.114.

95. See ibid. p.29.

96. Spivak, *In Other Worlds,* ed.cit. note 15, p.96.

97. See Eco, op.cit. note 45, pp.350–51. Eco sees Europe as remaining essentially polyglottal, with people speaking their own tongues, often not even learning others but being able to 'participate in [the] particular genius' of other languages.

98. Francois Rabelais, *Gargantua e Pantagruel* Book 2 ch.9.

99. Lewis Carroll, *The Hunting of the Snark,* Fit the Fourth: as in *The Complete Works of Lewis Carroll,* 1982, rpt. London: Chancellor Press, 1993, p.745.

100. Steiner, *After Babel,* ed. cit. note 46, p.292.

101. Robert J. Matthews, 'What Did Archimedes Mean by 'Χρυσός'?', *Difference in Translation,* ed.cit. note 1, p.54.

102. Walter Benjamin, op.cit. note 44, p.71.

Index